Liveable Lives

Liveable Lives

Living and Surviving LGBTQ Equalities in India and the UK

Niharika Banerjea and Kath Browne

BLOOMSBURY ACADEMIC
LONDON • NEW YORK • OXFORD • NEW DELHI • SYDNEY

BLOOMSBURY ACADEMIC
Bloomsbury Publishing Plc
50 Bedford Square, London, WC1B 3DP, UK
1385 Broadway, New York, NY 10018, USA
29 Earlsfort Terrace, Dublin 2, Ireland

BLOOMSBURY, BLOOMSBURY ACADEMIC and the Diana logo
are trademarks of Bloomsbury Publishing Plc

First published in Great Britain 2023

Copyright © Niharika Banerjea and Kath Browne, 2023

Niharika Banerjea and Kath Browne have asserted their right under the Copyright, Designs and Patents Act, 1988, to be identified as Authors of this work.

For legal purposes the Acknowledgements on p. xi constitute an extension of this copyright page.

Cover design: Adriana Brioso

This work is published open access subject to a Creative Commons Attribution-NonCommercial-NoDerivatives 4.0 International licence (CC BY-NC-ND 4.0, https://creativecommons.org/licenses/by-nc-nd/4.0/). You may re-use, distribute, and reproduce this work in any medium for non-commercial purposes, provided you give attribution to the copyright holder and the publisher and provide a link to the Creative Commons licence.

Bloomsbury Publishing Plc does not have any control over, or responsibility for, any third-party websites referred to or in this book. All internet addresses given in this book were correct at the time of going to press. The author and publisher regret any inconvenience caused if addresses have changed or sites have ceased to exist, but can accept no responsibility for any such changes.

A catalogue record for this book is available from the British Library.

Library of Congress Cataloging-in-Publication Data
Names: Banerjea, Niharika, author. | Browne, Kath, author.
Title: Liveable lives : living and surviving LGBTQ equalities in India and the UK / Niharika Banerjea and Kath Browne.
Description: New York : Bloomsbury Academic, an imprint of Bloomsbury Publishing, 2023. | Includes bibliographical references and index.
Identifiers: LCCN 2022055071 (print) | LCCN 2022055072 (ebook) | ISBN 9781350286771 (hardback) | ISBN 9781350286788 (paperback) | ISBN 9781350286795 (epub) | ISBN 9781350286801 (pdf) | ISBN 9781350286818
Subjects: LCSH: Sexual minorities–Great Britain. | Sexual minorities–India. | Equality–Great Britain. | Equality–India.
Classification: LCC HQ73.3.G7 B36 2023 (print) | LCC HQ73.3.G7 (ebook) | DDC 306.760941–dc23/eng/20230209
LC record available at https://lccn.loc.gov/2022055071
LC ebook record available at https://lccn.loc.gov/2022055072

ISBN:	HB:	978-1-3502-8677-1
	PB:	978-1-3502-8678-8
	ePDF:	978-1-3502-8680-1
	eBook:	978-1-3502-8679-5

Typeset by Integra Software Services Pvt. Ltd.
Printed and bound in Great Britain

To find out more about our authors and books visit www.bloomsbury.com and sign up for our newsletters.

This book is dedicated to all those across academia and activism who find and may find 'liveability' (with its translation and transliteration) useful to read and critique intersecting power relations that animate gendered and sexual(ized) lives.

Contents

List of figures	ix
List of table	x
Acknowledgements	xi

1 Introducing Liveable Lives 1
   Introduction 1
   Liveability: Why now? 2
   Liveability: Conceptual beginnings 5
   Researching liveability: Transnational-methodological
   parameters 17
   Outline of the book 28
   Note for (social science?) readers 31
   Concluding manoeuvres: Liveabilities through *Liveable Lives* 32

2 Liveability as a decolonial option through collaborative
   research and activisms 35
   Introduction 35
   Ourselves 38
   Coloniality and the figure of the 'Indian Queer' and
   'British Queer' 40
   Collaborative research 44
   Better than elsewhere? Geographical imaginings
   of 'other places' 56
   Conclusion 62

3 Structures of inclusion: Within and beyond sexualities and
   gender equalities and rights 65
   Introduction 65
   Implementing legislation: Living up to progress narratives? 66

	Postcolonial legalities: Recognition and rights in 'backward' states	70
	Hearts and minds are more than rights: Recognition and equality in India and the UK	75
	Mutual understanding and love, beyond same-sex marriage as the pinnacle of LG(BTQ) equalities?	84
	The complex significance of legislation	88
	Conclusion	91
4	What makes a life liveable? (Non)normative lives, ordinary lives	95
	Introduction	95
	'Flowing Upstream': Living and surviving/বেঁচে থাকা এবং টিকে থাকা (*benche thaka ebong tike thaka*/to live and to survive)	96
	The normative and non-normative/ নিয়মতান্ত্রিক এবং নিয়মবিরোধী (*Niyomtantrik ebong niyombirodhee*)	107
	The ordinary and the everyday/সাধারণ আর গতানুগতিক (*sadharon ar gotanugotik*)	115
	Conclusion	122
5	Performing liveabilities in Kolkata and Brighton: Creating new commonplaces	125
	Introduction	125
	Commonplace politics	127
	Practising commons, doing street theatre	130
	Performing liveabilities in Kolkata	132
	Performing liveabilities in Brighton	144
	Conclusion	150
Afterword		153
Notes		160
References		168
Index		184

Figures

1	Collage, Project Workshop, India	23
2	Collage, Project Workshop, England	23
3	Franco's map created in Project Workshop	59
4	England Project Workshop	105
5	Project Workshop, Kolkata	112
6	India Workshop	120

Table

1   Methods used in *Making Liveable Lives*   21

Acknowledgements

Thank you to all the participants and contributors who made *Liveable Lives* possible, we are deeply grateful for their critical words, images, affection and friendships.

Thank you Dr Nick McGlynn and Rukmini Banerjee whose research assistance and critical inputs were invaluable. To Dr Ranjita Biswas we owe a great debt in quietly holding our words and efforts throughout the project. To all members in Sappho for Equality who took special efforts to imagine that liveable lives are possible!

Thanks to Leela and Sumita for all their work and insights into the project, their Afterword and discussions about this book.

We are thankful to Stephanie Boulila for reading this manuscript and giving us valuable feedback.

Niharika is deeply grateful to University College Dublin for a six-month visiting fellowship to prepare this manuscript. Kath, I harbour a deep emotion and respect for you that keeps crossing boundaries to find home in critical collaborative discussions and writing. This book is an example of that. Thank you!

Kath would like to thank Niharika for her brilliance and perseverance. You show me what is possible in the most difficult of circumstances, and I feel lucky that you work with me. Thanks to Leela for working with me through two research projects. You are inspirational and insightful. Thank you.

1

Introducing Liveable Lives

Introduction

What is a liveable life?

জীবনের মতো জীবন কাকে বলে? (*Jeeboner mato jeebon kake bole?*)

What makes a life, life?

Liveable Lives explores these questions with Lesbian, Gay, Bi, Trans, and Queer (LGBTQ) identifying persons. How are LGBTQ lives desired and achievable (momentarily/temporally/spatially)? This book contests the deployment of hegemonic queer subjects to create forward/backward narratives of national progress with liveability at a particular historical moment of global sexual/gender inclusion. Contesting yet recognizing the place of legislations that liberalize sexual and gender rights, we contend that liveability needs to be a pivotal axis in analysing gender-sexual politics and their material manifestations.

Liveable Lives draws from our transnational project, *Making Liveable Lives: Rethinking Social Exclusion*,[1] a collaborative research work with Sappho for Equality, Kolkata,[2] and activists in Brighton, England (2014–16). It explored how LGBTQ identifying persons negotiate their lives to make them more liveable in their everyday living practices and desiring life within and beyond survival. This book argues for liveabilities' heterogeneous formations around LGBTQ equalities constituted through legal, social, political institutions and their enactments through everyday living. While it is tempting to define liveability from the outset, we did not do so in the project.

We follow this through and explore liveabilities through participants' narratives throughout the book, creating a multifarious exploratory conceptualization. This moves from using 'liveability' as a measurable concept towards a more multidimensional one, i.e. liveabilities.

Located in two institutions in Delhi and Dublin, writing this book together during the pandemic in 2021[3] has been a moment of doing theory transnationally while situated within critical empirical material. We start this chapter by outlining the need to talk about liveability within and beyond juridico-political[4] measures that include equalities legislation and political moves to create particular forms of social norms/orders, as a way to disrupt progress/backward narratives that are deployed to rank order countries according to the presence/absence of sexuality rights. Following that, drawing from the works of Judith Butler, we elaborate on the epistemological entry points to launch our consideration of the concept of liveability as we develop it through the critical empirical contexts that are the focus of this book. This segways into the transnational-methodological linkages in the following section. We start our engagement with the methodologies and methods that inform this book regarding our practice. The chapter ends with an outline of the book and notes for readers.

Liveability: Why now?

Thinking about liveability to speak about LGBTQ identifying lives enables engagements with living and desiring lives in ways that interrupt juridico-political assumptions of 'progress', which we disrupt as the sole and inevitable route towards a liveable life. These progress narratives create comparisons that underlie forward/backward temporal records in global sexual-gender politics. The *Making Liveable Lives* project looked at how different geographical, cultural spaces create and introduce liveabilities in the cracks and fissures of hegemonic gender-sexual practices and normative regimes. Our primary research objective was to explore how, when and where lives become liveable and not liveable across the two places. We see this as critical in creating liveabilities within and beyond juridico-political regimes, contesting the geopolitical hierarchies they underpin.

Sexual and gender identities play an increasingly important role in global political systems, including international human rights and development organizations. States in the Global North and international human rights and development organizations place nations within a worldwide democratic system by demonstrating inclusivity of LGBTQ populations through inclusive legislations (Banerjea et al., 2019; Browne et al., 2015; Rao, 2020). This feeds into 'assumptions of progress and the ideals and models that follow from understanding certain spaces and places as "leading the way" in terms of sexual and gender inclusions' (Browne et al., 2021: 4), such that particular trajectories of progress have shaped sexuality/gendered rights discourses since the early twenty-first century. Browne et al. (2021), speaking to scholarship in the area, underscore that such geographical imaginations 'often rely on the construction of a homogeneous and antediluvian Global South – an imagination that erases both the achievements of activists therein and the continued injustice, violence and oppression in what is imagined as the heartlands of progress in the metropolitan Global North' (5). There is then an 'outward flow of progress' from the north to the south, while at the same time, those from the south and situated within the north are presumed to pose a threat to such progress with their dead-end cultural practices (2021). At the same time, social groups and individuals associated with LGBTQ movements in the Global South often rhetorically connect their demands for rights to the imagination of a globally modern democratic state located elsewhere in the 'developed world'. Expressing anxieties about stepping 'backward' in a temporal logic of social justice, nation-states and social groups in their demands for rights (albeit in varied ways and for different reasons) can demonstrate aspirations to 'progress' into a favoured democratic league. Those who are unable to do so can face material consequences (see Banerjea & Browne, 2018; Boyce & Dasgupta, 2018; Boyce & Dutta, 2013; Browne et al., 2015; Rao, 2014).

Juridico-political legislative reforms, including equalities legislation around employment, same-sex marriage, adoption and parental rights, sexual and gendered progress, and an associated idea of freedom can be deemed the path to 'freedom' and liberation, to the liveable lives that are only available to some people, in some places. They are read as conditions in which sexual/gender agency is formulated through a linear temporal narrative based on particular contexts (Kulpa, 2014; Kulpa & Mizielińska, 2011). From the closet to the street, from the private to the public, from a condition of no equalities to full access to equal rights, these sets of temporal narratives are rooted in scaled geographical imaginings of advanced/backward nations. At the national level, they also become intelligible through tropes such as first world/third world, developed/underdeveloped and forward/backward. Sexual(ized) lives thus become rank ordered along with the countries in which they are situated through legislative markers through an inclusion (via legislative reform)/exclusion conceptual frame that does not foreground everyday lives. Lives are assumed to become unliveable because of the presence or absence of legal reforms, rather than engaging with how non-normative lives are lived.

Liveable Lives engages with lives that are both embedded and in between multiple realities that cross national, international, local, and embodied scales. Progressive legislation and judgements with imaginations of, and directives for, an inclusive social need to be continuously scrutinized (even while being celebrated) for their manifest and latent desires that reproduce post 9/11 geopolitical and hyper nationalist regimes. Drawing from decolonial analytics (Kulpa & Silva, 2016; Lugones, 2010; Mignolo, 2000, 2016), we interpret equalities and legislations as forms of rationalizing power that produce the 'colonial national-global subject'. Claims made to recognize this subject, within and across national territories, may either de-recognize caste-ed, raced and gender-based marginalizations (Boyce & Dasgupta, 2018) and/or have profound material implications for a politics of development. Another framing is needed to explore how lives are lived within and beyond juridico-political recognition and how these can be desired and limited to achieve liveabilities. Our work is thus an intervention; in asking what makes life liveable, we attempt to think with the participants to map how LGBTQ identifying persons live their lives within and between dynamic realities of normalizing legislation, everyday experiences of non-normative lives, and the desire for more/something else. We use this book to propose liveability as both an academic and activist tool that foregrounds the question of what makes a life, life, and how can this be worked towards?

Liveability: Conceptual beginnings

Jyoti: If what makes life liveable seem so far away as to be fantasy, does that realisation make life less liveable anyway [laughs]?

(In-depth interview, India)

Charlie: I think the line's very fine [between living and surviving]. What I was trying to say earlier is I think the line is also about the attitude I take towards someone. So if I take a forgiving and gentler attitude, things become liveable, which didn't feel liveable before. So I think the older I've got, the more I've felt that how I approach things makes a huge difference to whether they feel liveable, bearable, survivable, whatever to me. But it's not natural language to me. It's not the way that I would normally speak, but I could see the usefulness of it.

(Project Workshop, England)

Liveability as a conceptual tool holds the possibility to move the discourse of sexuality/gendered rights beyond juridico-political equalities of sexualities/genders. While the decolonial aspects of this statement will be discussed in the next chapter, we highlight the epistemological usefulness of the concept in this introductory chapter. Joyti facilitates the concrete grounding of the term in two senses. First, a liveable life/জীবনের মতো জীবন (*Jeeboner mato jeebon*/A life that is like a life) may reside in the fantastic and in the material every day at the same time (both lived and desired). Even if it does reside in the fantastic, that does not mean that life becomes less liveable; indeed, desiring the 'fantasy' and striving for it may make life more liveable (see Chapter 4). Second, this dual impression allows us to ground liveability in lived experiences, with its attendant desires. Lived experience, following Joan Scott (2013), is that which engages with the particularities of the ordinary, the routine, to develop an adjustment, critique, and coming into being. These are created through the second excerpt through the interplay between living and surviving and questionable separation/juxtapositioning of the two (we develop this through considerations of ordinariness below and in Chapter 4). The place of liveability in one's speech, as the participant points out, is not part of one's 'natural language' and brings in difficulties of translation as well. To begin then, we will take a brief tour of our reading of Judith Butler's work. Following that, we draw attention to the question of ordinary to add a related epistemological parameter that we will develop throughout the book.

Butler and a liveable life

We owe our conceptual debt for *Liveable Lives* to Judith Butler's articulation of 'what makes a life liveable' (Butler, 2004a, 2004b). We use her work to explore *liveable lives* as a platform and a base. Throughout the research project on which this book draws from, we have used the spelling 'liveable' rather than Butler's 'livable'. Where we refer to Butler's and others' development of this concept, we use their spelling. Using the 'e' indicates our focus on lives, materialities and contexts, building from the existing theoretical insights. In charting a course through this body of work and maintaining the focus, this section considers discussions of precarity, recognition and inclusion that pertain directly to our considerations of liveable lives.

Butler's articulation of livability is connected to her concerns about precariousness, questions of precarity, and vulnerability and grievability, all of which preoccupy much of her work around ethics, politics and resistance (Butler, 2004a, 2009, 2015). In contrast to precariousness as an existential condition, precarity points to a politically induced condition. Vulnerability can mean a material state wherein one is exposed to bodily harm or injury. At the same time, it is part of a symbolic order that precedes a social group and guides their practices, roles and expressions. Therefore, people can be vulnerable precisely because their gendered and sexual lives come into being through such symbolic orders. In contrast to an existential, subjective and politically induced condition, vulnerability is 'a relation to a field of objects, forces, and passions that impinge upon or affect us in some way' (Butler, Gambetti & Sabsay, 2016: 25). Vulnerability and precarity – in their interrelationship – can frame the im/possibilities of what constitutes a liveable life, through regulatory norms of recognizability that determine who is worthy of recognition and who is not. So, Butler states:

> When we ask what makes a life liveable, we are asking about certain normative conditions that must be fulfilled for life to become life.
> (Butler, 2004b: 39)

Those who do not conform to the normative scripts of sex and gender are 'abject', unviable and often relegated to the domain of space that is not liveable. In other words, those vulnerable lives that are not '"recognisable" as "human" are more precarious than those who are' (Lloyd, 2015: 217). Norms then both facilitate and restrict lives by both enabling and limiting the possibilities of what constitutes a liveable life. As Butler says:

> Sometimes a normative conception of gender can undo one's personhood, undermining the capacity to persevere in a livable life.
> (Butler, 2004b: 2)

While Butler argues that liveability is intimately linked to the stability of recognition through identity categories, at the same time, she also writes that the inflexibility of such naming categories imposes constraints on life itself and can paradoxically make it unliveable. Hence, talking of norms and conventions that can both facilitate and restrict lives, Butler writes:

> What is most important is to cease legislating for all lives what is livable only for some, and similarly, to refrain from proscribing for all lives what is unlivable[5] for some.
> (Butler, 2004b: 8)

In addition, Butler is clear that not all may seek inclusion in the same way to counter the violence in creating and enforcing normativities. In other words, if I am outside the normative grid, my life may be made not liveable; but I may also choose to live without recognition, as I may see the terms of recognition as too restrictive. In such cases, the terms by which recognition is conferred may make my life not liveable, and I may thus choose not to be recognized at all. Recognition is, therefore, 'double-edged':

> I want to maintain that legitimisation is doubled-edged: it is crucial that politically we claim intelligibility and recognisability; and it is crucial politically that we maintain a critical and transformative relation to the norms that govern what will and will not count as an intelligible and recognisable alliance and kinship.
> (Butler, 2004b: 117)

As we argue in Chapter 3, legislation and juridico-political conditions that account for and enable sexual/gender inclusions as forms of state recognition are essential and limited simultaneously. This tension and complexity are crucial to our conception of liveabilities. In relating liveability to critical considerations of the centrality of legal reforms, it is important to note that the conditions for life for Butler are embedded in the social within and beyond legislation. As she states:

> There is not life without the conditions of life that sustain life, and those conditions are pervasively social, establishing not the discrete ontology of the person, but rather the interdependency of persons, involving reproducible and sustaining social relations, and relations to the environment and to non-human forms of life, broadly considered.
>
> (Butler, 2009: 19)

Liveability thus is not based on an ontological right bearing human subject, precisely because an 'individual life' is exposed to differential forms of precarity. Life is relational. What does a life need to be life is not only a juridical question but deeply bounded by a sociality that also exceeds the normalizations of legislative recognition. Then, the purpose for us is not to create criteria of a 'good life' but to explore the possibilities of liveable lives within and beyond juridical questions. Such a purpose at a political level expands considerations of liveability as a political concept:

> That illustrates the operations of different modes of power – such as cisgenderism, heteronormativity, racism, and ableism – that draw the line between those populations that are understood as valuable, and therefore livable, and those that are not.
>
> (Karhu, 2022: 307)

It allows for more than the problematics of normalizations, prejudices and exclusions also to consider:

> What would make trans, nonbinary, and genderqueer lives more livable against the backdrop of cisnormativity and the history of violent discrimination and marginalisation of LGBTIQ lives.
>
> (Karhu, 2022: 309)

Seeing liveability in this vein then extends considerations of sexual and gendered politics that have often noted not only the limits of judicial rights but operate/d outside of them to seek more than changes in legislations and state inclusions, contesting the state as a form of oppression that reiterates heteronormative ideals (Stychin, 2003). Demands such as holding hands in early gay liberation movements in the Anglo-American world and questioning state normalizations that create material precarity or seeking ordinary lives that question current normativities have long been a feature of queer/LGBTQ activist and academic work. As Gavin Brown notes:

> The really profound changes in the people's intimate lives have been the result of the cumulative changes in the everyday practices of millions of people, gay and straight. To lead an openly gay life is now more mundane than transgressive.
> (Brown, 2012: 1068)

Although not named as liveability, the idea of everyday materialities and lives as central political questions is not new.[6] Our discussions of liveabilities build on engagements with everyday life's sexual and gendered politics to consider the normalizations that constitute not/liveable lives and the desire for these within and beyond juridico-political frames as an activist and academic work.

Beyond inclusion/exclusion

Our conceptualizations of liveabilities move beyond the either/or of legislative inclusion or social exclusion. The inclusion/exclusion frame is rooted in intersecting racialized, casteist, gendered and classed imaginations of local, national and global citizenship that reproduces an ideal national-sexual subject. Such a binary also does not hold when considerations of homonormativity are fundamental to contemporary engagements with sexual and gendered politics;

yet, this binary rarely comes under detailed scrutiny. As has been shown, the ideals of inclusion are contested through scholarship and activisms that show that inclusion legislatively or through mainstream queer cultures is limited, partial and exclusionary (Browne & Bakshi, 2013; Duggan, 2003; Richardson, 2004, 2005; Warner, 1999a, 1999b). An inclusion/exclusion binary cannot capture lives and forms of living that reside both *within and outside* juridico-political frames of intelligibility. At the same time, while recognizing the normalizing impulses of legislative inclusion, we also want to explore their possibilities. Conversely, in emphasizing the limits of these very inclusions, we seek to move beyond them. Striving for inclusion as the opposite of exclusion is thus problematic, and liveability offers another framework and different political goals.

Liveability can counter the inclusion/exclusion binary as a concept and political aim by reorientating the focus towards what makes a life, life. While there have been significant discussions of the political import of liveability and recognition (see Kallock, 2018; Karhu, 2022), there has been less of a focus on the lived experiences of those who are otherwise judicially unintelligible and abject, as well as those who are supposedly recognized and 'sorted'. Place can play a crucial role in assigning the categories of abject/sorted to various bodies, or not. Liveability can serve to disrupt these assumptions. In places where juridical recognition is guaranteed, liveability can facilitate discussions about the forms of living that recognize the limitations of this recognition. It can be used to question assumptions of liveabilities that supposedly arrive from legal inclusions. Hence, it allows us both inside *and* outside, inside-outside, the realms of legal rationality. Taking this stand does more than refuse the sole location of liveabilities within 'progressive' nations. It fundamentally questions the supposedly geopolitical neutralities of the inclusion/exclusion logic based on equalities underlying juridico-political regimes. Liveability explored through lived experiences allows insights and access into forms of living that escape and/or exceed such place-based categorizations and homogeneities. In *Liveable Lives* empirically investigating liveabilities, specifically in two contexts where legislative recognition has been achieved and where it was not at the time of the project work (2015/16), we explore the importance of being recognized in law, but also the limitations of this, analysing how lives are made liveable beyond legal recognition. Scholarly engagement with the idea of liveability is thus central to this work, as is its usefulness for collective social action and imagining queer futures.

Desiring liveability, desiring ordinary

Ordinariness emerges from thinking through the everyday. It can threaten or subvert the normative when this includes acts such as 'holding hands', 'kissing in public' and other contestations of Brahmanical and heteropatriarchal norms. For instance, the materialities of same-sex couples holding hands reflect the ideal of doing something that others (who are also racialized/class/aged/embodied in particular ways) take for granted. It recognizes that transgression can lead to the installation of an ordinary state of affairs without necessarily embracing/replicating the hetero/homonormative (Browne & Bakshi, 2013). The 'kiss of love', a youth-led campaign consisting of publicly visible kissing to protest moral policing in urban places, occupied a few metro cities in India from late 2014 to early 2015.[7] In this way, ordinariness as a political intention moves between the transgression/assimilation binary and asks instead what it might mean to 'be ordinary' without sliding into normativity (Browne & Bakshi, 2013).

In *Liveable Lives*, we bring the question of liveability into conversation with the ordinary. This serves as a critical lens to understand the minutiae of navigations involved to make life worth living within and against the lived realities including gender, sexualities, race, class, ethnicity, caste and location. These micro-efforts cannot always be assimilated within critiques of normalizations. Normalization, as Browne and Bakshi argue, implies the following:

> ... falling in line with a norm, an accepted way of being and living in a community. It relies on particular standards or norms, which here, only some can achieve or at least approximate. Inclusion through normalisations, such as that instigated through legislative measures, can mean that people are excluded in various ways, outside or at least on the edge, and marginalised.
>
> (2013: 190)

Ordinariness can be equated with normativity, and eradicating difference has been critiqued by those who worry about the conditionalities of making sexual difference not matter (Richardson & Monro, 2012). This, it is argued, leads from and into assimilationist impulses that are 'based on the idea that LGBT people are just like everyone else' (Santos, 2012: 156). However, these critiques of normal lives relate to the pursuit of normal through normativities, juxtaposed with the transgressive, which is celebrated, because it is set up through the dichotomy of normal/transgressive. In contrast, the desire to be part of the fabric of the city (Browne & Bakshi, 2013), wanting acceptance within families the struggle to blend in to avoid violative behaviour (Biswas et al., 2019) and the need to feel normal in one's body (Biswas et al., 2019) within cis/heteronormative worlds work beyond this binary and ask for different considerations. Such desires and attendant efforts cannot be read as assimilative or as necessarily unremarkable. They can be both, but they might not be.

There is potential in ordinary challenges to the everyday that escape normalization, even when tilting towards becoming normal because there is power in the mundane. Eli Clare's queer crip theory/activist work speaks of feeling ordinary and familiar without seeking to replicate hegemonic values to make him normal:

> Our bodies as ordinary and familiar: this idea flies in the face of the gawkers and bashers who try to shape us as inspirational and

heroic, tragic and pitiful, perverse and unnatural. We don't get to simply be ordinary and familiar very often. And when it does happen, it is such a relief, so rare and wonderful. Don't mistake me: I don't mean that we need to find normal and make it our own. Normal – that center against which everyone of us is judged and compared: in truth I want us to smash it to smitherines. And in its place, celebrate our irrevocably different bodies, our queerness, our crip lives, telling stories and creating for ourselves an abiding sense of the ordinary and familiar.

(Clare, 2002: NP)

Clare highlights the creative possibilities of being ordinary and familiar, contesting readings of desiring ordinariness as necessarily eradicating differences and those that equate ordinariness with normalizations and normativities. Clare thus seeks to open up a form of politics that moves away from normalizations without negating ordinariness. Yet, differences still matter. As Clare notes, differences can be celebrated in their irrevocability as they become ordinary in particular spatial-temporal moments. Some might not want to be the same, but they also desire not to be persecuted, oppressed, excluded and othered. Ordinariness then need not be achieved through normalizations or attendant conditionalities. There might be a desire to walk through streets without being noticed, differences not erased but also not remarkable or reactions to them fear inducing. This can be a political aim that does not require adherence to specific forms of recognition.

In returning to Butler, liveability can be read as residing as an ordinary aspiration in her work, through what she calls a 'normative commitment to equality'. In this, she discusses 'food, shelter, work, medical care, education, right to mobility and expression, protection against injury and oppression' (2009: 28–9). This normative commitment is required to do away with the conditions that create precarity. As a politically induced condition (Butler, 2009), precarity enhances the vulnerabilities of everyday life. Access to food, shelter, clothing, healthcare, education, livelihood is a social fact of everyday life, and hence there is an individual and collective stake in these resources. Drawing from *Undoing Gender*, Rushing locates liveability as a normative/ordinary aspiration within an 'ability to live and breathe and move,' i.e. 'a life that should be allowed to breathe, persist, and be recognised' (2010: 291).

The normativity of Butler's liveability is an aspiration and, as Rushing (2010) suggests, is different from a proscription. Hence, Butler never delineates specific norms under which such conditions can be ensured but lays them down in abstract terms, connecting it to a realm of possibility. Possibility thus differentiates normative aspiration from the normalized normative state of being. It can be a desire, a fantasy. Hence for us, liveability is not anti-normative – a critique made against Butler's concept (Rushing, 2010) – but instead implies an 'ethical and political demand on those with power to refuse recognition to certain others' and an expansion of the 'human to be' (Rushing, 2010: 292, 298). Where normative frames underly the heterosexual matrix, in temporal and spatially specific contexts, it affects access to resources and thus the ability to live a liveable life. A 'normative commitment to equality' then becomes a struggle for ordinary things in the minutiae of the everyday. The ordinary then conceived through liveability is both political and a movement towards something desired, contests regulatory norms, and offers possibilities of elsewheres.

Yet, ordinary lifeworlds are not to be read unquestioningly as authentic or existing outside of normalization tendencies. They are spheres of sociality that are place based. The normalized 'ordinary nature' of discrimination and violence within the family, public space, and healthcare systems that create the conditions for seeking liveable lives as political acts is part of the (re)creation of hierarchical differences. The move to develop alternatives to being included in seeking gender and sexual liberations results in meaningful and necessary considerations of creating transgressions and spaces that desire to be different to the norm or mainstream. And yet, the struggle to remain different to the norm is braided with a sensibility of ordinariness that exceeds our understanding of what inclusion means and escapes critiques of homonormativity and normalizations (see Chapter 4). Thus, perhaps a desire or some desires for ordinariness can be read as ethical orientations that need to allow for critique (as reproducing normalized and oppressive structures), and also holding potential for change.

In bringing together the language and experiences of the ordinary lifeworlds of our participants (see Chapter 4), we run the concept of liveability through 'textures of the ordinary' (Das, 2020). In her work on 'ordinary ethics', Veena Das talks about the ordinary as a sphere within which subjects become moral by orienting themselves within the everyday (Das, 2012: 134). Speaking from her thirty years of ethnographic work with urban poor communities in resettlement colonies in Delhi, Das deploys the ordinary to point to various micro-histories and micro-geographies of living that may otherwise be dismissed as '*too* quotidian' to count for ethical behaviour (138). She locates ethics in the minutiae of the 'normative practices of everyday life' and in the 'small acts that allow life to be knitted together pair by pair' (138–9). What might otherwise be dismissed as habitual, repetitive and routine for Das also contains an orientation towards the ethical, as a way of residing in the world from which 'doubts, despair, disorders, and improvisations occur' (2020: 66). The act of residing is different from rule-following, involving subtle gestures, dispositions, acknowledgement (and its withholding), timely exchange of gifts, modes of concealment, even small acts of survival, all of which are part of the maintenance of 'forms of life' (102). Das suggests that all of these can be read as 'critical for understanding how everyday life might provide the therapy for the very violation that has grown from within it' (117). In Chapter 4, we will bring our participants conversations around liveability together with the premise that an ontological understanding of the concept, and by implication a universalized meter of legal reforms, is futile. We consider the usefulness of the term 'liveability', with its Bangla transliterations of জীবনের মতো জীবন (*jeeboner mato jeebon*/life worth living), ভাল থাকা *(bhalo thaka/ staying well)*[8] relating to desires and expectations that circulate in social lives, as LGBTQ people told us. In Chapter 5, we extend our reading of ordinariness through a consideration of 'commonplace'. This builds on questioning the juridico-political inclusions/exclusions (Chapter 3) through explorations that recognize that move from in place/out of place to in Chapter 5 places that can be created 'in common' in ways that can contest normativities, recognizing differences. In this way, the book works to develop understandings of liveabilities through engaging with the possibilities and limits of juridico-political regimes beyond inclusion/exclusion (Chapter 3), ordinariness (Chapter 4) and the creation of moments of commonplace (Chapter 5). It does so through transnational empirical research, to which we now turn.

Researching liveability: Transnational-methodological parameters

To undertake the work of exploring what makes lives liveable for LGBTQ people, we adopted a transnational feminist queer methodological approach. We avoided comparative research that seeks sameness and difference among places under study and rejected the assumption that objectivity and rigour are desirable by not creating comparable data. Comparative analysis can create 'winners' and 'losers' (deliberately or inadvertently). Instead, we focused on developing understandings of what makes life liveable for LGBTQ people through tools that worked for those places, which were developed through transnational dialogues between academics and activists across Brighton, Kolkata, Evansville and Delhi.[9] In doing so, we create theory across places by exploring how liveabilities are understood and imagined within specific national contexts and through transnational activist/academic engagements that question comparative geopolitical hierarchies of forward/backward states. Here we outline the transnational formation of the research before giving insight into the study sites and then describe the methods used.

We deployed transnational research as a methodology that moves beyond working with participants in various places and/or following through different sites, i.e. not as a multi-sited ethnographic practice (Falzon, 2016; Marcus, 2011). Our work creates transnational pieces of knowledge through collaborative research with activists and academics in different places. We refused to impose Global North ideals/values where the south is a data set for theorizing in the north, refiguring traditional power configurations around the researcher (north)/researched (south) binary. Instead, we developed networks and gathered narratives in both places creating transnational theorizing for rethinking assumptions regarding progress/backwardness concerning LGBTQ activisms and lives (see Chapter 2). In our work, researchers based in England did not do participatory research in India and then went back to write. Indian activists and researchers co-designed methods and theorized together with English-based researchers drawing on data from both places and exploring the particularities of each location. Travel only went one way, researchers from India travelling to Brighton to share their expertise in conducting street theatre (see Chapter 5) and creating a project video.[10]

Throughout *Liveable Lives*, we do not engage in an examination of the transnational production of homophobia and its local linkages or follow the afterlife of colonial legislation (Rao, 2014, 2020), but instead specifically engage with narratives of living across two nations, connected to the other through long imperial histories of colonization. Their relationality and hierarchization both underpin and do not form the primary lens through which we explore what makes lives liveable. In doing so, we argue for a decolonial understanding of LGBTQ lives.

We chose India and Great Britain (Northern Ireland did not legalize same-sex marriage until 2020) to investigate LGBTQ liveabilities due to their ongoing economic, social and cultural connections and legislative differences in the realm of LGBTQ equalities. In Scotland, England and Wales, same-sex marriage was passed in 2014, following the wide-ranging UK-wide Equality Act in 2010. The Equality Act can be seen as the culmination of over a decade of legislative change, in part driven by the EU and the European Court of Human Rights, and Great Britain is seen as one of the 'most advanced' countries concerning LGBTQ legislative equalities. At the time of this project work, in India, conversely, Section 377 of the Indian Penal Code (S 377) criminalized 'carnal intercourse against the order of nature'. S 377 has its origins in an 1860 British colonial law. The Delhi High Court read it down in the Naz Foundation vs Government of NCT of Delhi case on 2 July 2009, but the Supreme Court reinstated it in December 2013.[11] In metrics and comparisons which seek to identify places as 'LGBTQ-friendly', legislation emerges as a critical form of evidence (Browne et al., 2015). While Great Britain is generally seen as a world leader in terms of LGBTQ equalities and legislation, India is rated poorly in metrics of LGBTQ equalities due in no small part to this legislative context. Indeed, decriminalization and subsequent recriminalization have been used to describe it as one of the 'most homophobic countries' ahead of countries where homosexuality remains punishable by death (Batchelor, 2017; Nunez, 2017; Strasser, 2014). We sought to challenge some of the conclusions that we might draw from a focus on legislation, namely the comparison between the Great Britain and India that places sexual and gender politics 'over there' (in India and often by extension the Global South) where we are 'losing', and frames 'us here' (in Great Britain, and often the Global North) as 'sorted' and 'winning'.[12] The concept of liveability enables us to open up and critique how LGBTQ politics can frame specific contexts, such as India, as 'backward' and failing, in contrast to other contexts, such as Great Britain understood as progressing due to recent legislative equalities.

These place-based specificities shaped the research design (however, more nuance around specificities within national contexts is required). Practically, this meant a research design developed collaboratively, with shared research questions, but implemented differently in India and England.[13] The framing and choice of methods were made organically. Given that the primary intent was to develop theory between the team in India and England and show how different liveabilities are produced that disrupt Global North/ Global South divides in sexuality rights discourse, the methods ran through several iterations before we could come to a consensus. There is no correct method to intervene in debates that hierarchize 'Western democracies' as spaces of inclusion, vilifying exotic 'others' as 'inherently homophobic', synonymous with 'backward'. The particular methods were designed to create conditions to bring individuals, groups and teams in and between India and England into dialogue. This underlay our methodological transnational collaboration and contextualization. Table 1 lists the methods developed collaboratively and used in the *Liveable Lives* project.

The methods were deployed in geographically sensitive ways that accounted for what was key to responding to the research questions by the academic/activist researchers in each place. A conscious decision was taken not to standardize them across places, instead of allowing the place to dictate the method in ways that sought to explore lives in these places on their terms. For example, project workshops were developed, which ran differently in each country and managed by academic and activist researchers both in and across the respective countries. The analysis was undertaken jointly after drawing out themes through two face-to-face meetings and regular Skype meetings where meanings, interpretations and implications of the narratives and data were discussed, allowing us to contest the forward/backward understanding of sexualities.

Table 1 Methods used in *Making Liveable Lives*.

Method	Description	Place
Project Workshops	Five workshops with 94 LGBTQ identifying participants: • individual interviews and group discussions (n. 29) • mapmaking (n. 43) • lifelines (n. 13) • collages, posters and illustrations (n. 20) • free writing (n. 12 + a collaborative multi-workshop scroll)	England: Brighton x1, Southampton x1, Leicester x1, Hull x2
Project Workshops	Forty-three LBT identifying participants • individual interviews and group discussions (n. 6) • lifelines (n. 35) • collages, posters and illustrations (n. 33)	Siliguri x1, Kolkata x2, Kolkata surrounding area x2
Individual interviews	26 in-depth with LBT identifying persons	West Bengal, India
Liveable Lives website	145 LGBTQ identifying persons engaged via: • Five online surveys (n. 115) • Online discussion forum (n. 141) • Pictures and photos (n. 87)	Great Britain/India

Method	Description	Place
Street theatre workshops with performances	Six events with thirty-five LGBTQ Identifying persons	Kolkata/Brighton
Desk-based reviews	• Review of global indices relating to LGBTQ equalities (Browne et al., 2015) • Review of media discussion of LGBTQ rights and legislation in India • Review of the implementation of equalities legislation in England and Wales (Browne et al., 2016)	Global/India/ England and Wales

This approach allowed us to move beyond standardization and comparison, finding better/worse places to live as a 'sexually divergent' being. In our various discussions, legislation, while important, was not the primary lens through which we engaged with our participants. Hence, different kinds of personal and collective realities were shared. We would like to particularly draw attention to two of the above methods that helped us move beyond the comparative framing, i.e. the street theatre and performances (Chapter 5) and the collage making. Figures 1 and 2 are examples of collage making as a mode of storytelling, weaving thoughts around living together to communicate what makes one's life liveable. We intersperse these throughout our book as our archives of liveability, a part of one's queer material culture. Magazines sold in each place were given to participants. These were 'mainstream' magazines made into symbolic photomontages to create a narrative of liveability and words sparingly juxtaposed. They offer creative and verbal/nonverbal interventions using normative magazines and contesting them in ways that seek to articulate responses to the question – 'what makes life liveable for LGBTQ people?'

Introducing Liveable Lives 23

Figure 1 Collage, Project Workshop, India. Image: Author's own.

Figure 2 Collage, Project Workshop, England. Image: Author's own.

Translating liveability

As part of a transnational research and activist team, translation was primary. We refused to define liveability and fold it into a pre-given set of research methods from the start. To openly explore what liveability might mean for LGBTQ people within and beyond the conceptualizations of livability in the literature, we stepped away from setting a perimeter around the term with a set of fixed factors. Instead, we attempted to open up and understand the concept through what participants shared with us. This was the case in both India and England.

The process of isolating the themes around liveability was twofold, one of which happened before the interviews and the project workshops and one after. Before we began the interviews and project workshops, we discussed amongst ourselves what kind of questions may elicit an understanding of what is a liveable life for LGBTQ people, জীবনের মতো জীবন কাকে বলে? (*Jeeboner mato jeebon kake bole*/What makes life a life)? After all, not all participants would identify with the term 'liveability' – even in its transliterated state – and then we may have diverse answers even if they did. The India research team did not linearly conceive transliterations, but they emerged during the project workshops. So in India, we collectively decided to ask questions about one's life and living, in addition, to directly asking how they would understand liveability and survival, বেঁচে থাকা এবং টিকে থাকা (*benche thaka ebong tike thaka*/ to live and to survive), further breaking it down into জীবনের মতো জীবন (*jiboner mato jibon*/ life worth living), ভাল থাকা এবং খারাপ থাকা (*bhalo thaka ebong kharap thaka*/staying well and staying unwell). This yielded a rich array of conversations and life stories, emerging from a person's unique history and context across different spaces and institutional settings. In England, the project workshops asked two key questions:

As an LGBTQ person:

1. What makes your life liveable?
2. What makes your life not liveable?

These were printed on blank pieces of paper, put on the walls and asked in group and individual interviews. They were further explored through the questions and prompts that delved into places, people and times where life was more/less liveable, feelings when life is liveable or not and fitting in.

Following the period of fieldwork and data collection in India, Sappho for Equality thematically arranged vital insights into a research report (Biswas et al., 2016), exclusively focusing on field data collected with LBT persons in West Bengal, to document and detail different aspects of what it means to live and survive with and beyond legislative reforms. Simultaneously, the research team in England prepared an Equalities Legislation report which critically explored local government engagements with Equalities legislation in England and Wales (Banerjea et al., 2019, chapter 4; Browne et al., 2016). Although the reports were place specific with particular interventions desired (local government action in England and Wales, awareness and understanding and recognition in West Bengal), these reports were not written in geographical isolation. While the research teams in Brighton and Kolkata took the lead in preparing the reports, extensive discussions and inputs were shared between them to create the final versions. Throughout this process and other analyses and writing, we have intended to disrupt monotonous narratives of forward and backward states while simultaneously moving away from presenting thematic universals about liveability. These motivations underlay our exchanges and created the research, analyses and outputs. In this book, whilst we draw on the data, we build from these analyses to undertake a deeper conceptual exploration into liveable lives. To that end, we work with 'partial truths' that help us open up the concept of liveability from meanings derived from living as LGBTQ identified persons in India and England. In this way, liveability was moved from the conceptual/political framings in the literature to what these might mean to LGBTQ people and their lives. This book uses this to re-interrogate the concept through the participants' stories and related insights that we gained in the project.

Translating LGBTQ

We use LGBTQ throughout this book as a deliberate way to engage with this global category head on, with the tool of liveability. In no way is the term meant to erase and/or dominate the rich histories of non-normative sexual and gendered lives that exceed the LGBTQ category in either English or Bangla. In Chapter 2, we explore decolonial considerations of liveabilities. In this chapter, we note our use of LGBTQ, recognizing postcolonial critiques that have challenged the universal circulation of 'LGBTQ' by pointing out the limitations, occlusions and usefulness[14] of LGBTQ. LGBT and other terms to describe identities and sexualities have long been contested in queer thinking within the Global North. Yet despite or perhaps creating these critiques, these terms circulate within a globalized network of rights discourses, aid and development and allow NGOs and groups to claim funding for health intervention, visibility and anti-discrimination policies at various scales of globalizing states and local law enforcement agencies. At the same time, this circulation flattens out place-specific categorizations, allowing only selective groups who have the social and cultural resources to enter the globalizing circuits (Dutta, 2013; Dutta & Roy, 2014).

It has long been recognized that using identity categorizations such as LGBTQ is problematic and can be necessary for engaging participants who use these terms to understand themselves, organize and create community (Browne & Nash, 2010). This project was more than engaging people with whom we could speak and also about using this acronym to enable transnational discussions and make intelligible the global narratives of progress and backward states in the sexuality rights discourse (Browne, Banerjea et al., 2015, see also Chapter 2). Our decision to use LGBTQ to describe our work and its attendant translatability is immersed in the complex realities of the limitations of categories of identities and Global North/Global South power relations. It also masks the differential use of terms deployed to undertake the research.

In the UK, through advertisements in social media, LGBT media, emails to organizations, personal contacts and word of mouth, we recruited participants to project workshops (in England) and online surveys (which were open to all across the UK). We used the term LGBTQ working across LGBT as this was the norm at the point of the fieldwork and data collection and including Q to recognize those who identified as queer/questioning. Any exclusion would have been seen as 'cutting out a part of the community', and in the latter part of the decade, exclusions have been contentiously deployed against transpeople as part of the LGBT collective.

In India, 'LBTQ' was either used independently or with related Bangla terms such as সমকামী (*samakamee*/a person who desires the same) and রূপান্তরকামী (*roopantorkamee*/a person desiring change). The absence of the G in India related to the groups that Sappho for Equality worked with, the gendered differentiation that means different forms of access to opportunity structures, and the separate histories of struggle for gender variant persons. The two English terms 'lesbian' and 'transman' were also commonly used to self-identify. A few participants did not use any self-identifying term but focused entirely on talking about desire, love and their bodies. We also use terms not commonly used in the Global North deliberately to challenge these hierarchies and dominance – such as LB, which is used in India to mean lesbian or sometimes lesbian and bisexual – contesting the divisions that can emerge between these identities in places like Great Britain/Global North (Hemmings, 2002, 2007; Maliepaard, 2015, 2017, 2020).

We used LGBTQ because in Great Britain, these terms were heavily used, and in India, they were already in circulation due to either NGO-ization and/or films. We see liveability – that has been conceptualized and now circulated (by us) – lying somewhere between these different scalar usages of LGBTQ. Thus, while we do run the risk of reproducing the discourse that we seek to interrupt, deploying the LGBTQ acronym, in our work, it is also meant to produce and make visible some archives that otherwise get dissipated in the progress/backward narratives to which it is typically attached. In keeping with this intention, therefore, while using the acronym LGBTQ, this book simultaneously refuses to categorize participants when sharing excerpts of their words and visuals archived in workshops, interviews, websites, social media and street theatre performances. Those who narrated and shared their thoughts, images and experiences do not inhabit this book as universalized sexual/gendered beings but as subjects who, while tagged with or claiming to be LGBTQ, can exist within and outside of this acronym. Therefore, we would request the readers of this book to read our participants and us as textured sexual/gendered subjects who narrate our lives and the possibilities of making them (more) liveable in ordinary ways. In doing so, we move towards an anti-essentialist reading of LGBTQ liveabilities.

Outline of the book

Beginning our considerations of the significance of legislative reforms to the constitution of sexual identities, expressions and practices and the division, aid and material development of nation-states, in Chapter 2, we explore the decolonial lens of liveability. In particular, we explore and contest the forward/backward critiques of LGBTQ juridico-political measures of progress. This chapter further underpins the empirical chapters, both conceptually and their place-based relationalities. We explore how Great Britain/India are positioned relationally in broader contexts of Global North/ Global South hierarchies around sexual liberations and inclusions, positioning ourselves within and beyond the Indian Queer/British Queer and exploring their power-laden inter-relationalities around sexual and gender equalities. We argue for liveability's decolonial potential to explore lives that can be juridically unintelligible because of hetero/homonormative nationalistic normalizations. We further the methodological framing of liveable lives introduced here to understand the contestations of hierarchies and inclusion/exclusion binaries inherent in the framings of the UK/India. We finish the chapter exploring how participants recreated the imaginings of 'other places'. Focusing on Great British participants, we explore their imaginings of other places as more dangerous and less liveable for LGBT people than the 'here'. In doing so, we show the macro-ways in which Global North/Global South are conceptualized by Great British, predominantly English, participants and urban/rural by Bengali participants offering decolonial critiques of these imaginings.

Chapter 3 explores the place of juridico-political structures that create a form of rationalizing power circulating within systems of law, courts and law enforcement agencies, which produce and mark the rights-bearing subject. Contesting both inclusion/exclusion and here/there narratives, the chapter empirically investigates the limitations and import of equalities legislation and associated rights seemingly assigned to all citizens. It begins with an exploration of the local government implementation of the Equality Act 2010, noting how local governments failed to enact the legislation and associated guidance, in this way questioning the necessary links between legislation and practice. Moving to India, we use a media analysis to illustrate the import that legal reforms can have and the changes seen in the media that track changes in court decisions regarding S 377. Using British and Bengali participants' views and experiences, we highlight the limitations of legislative change, including around same-sex marriage. This chapter highlights the complexities of recognition, as participants seek not to overturn marriage of legislative gains but also question their place in happiness and liveability. Yet, Bengali participants also told us of their import, speaking to their significance and activisms that demanded more than legislative inclusions. For some, such activisms kept them alive.

Chapter 4 explores liveabilities through the everyday, moving from engagements with national legislation. We consider the conceptual schemas of living and surviving/বেঁচে থাকা এবং টিকে থাকা (*benche thaka ebong tike thaka*/to live and to survive), the normative and non-normative/নিয়মতান্ত্রিক এবং নিয়মবিরোধী (*Niyomtantrik ebong niyombirodhee*) and the ordinary and the everyday/সাধারণ আর গতানুগতিক (*sadharon ar gotanugotik*), including its attendant material and discursive realities. Deploying a liveability lens allows us to focus on those ways of life and living that 'exceed normative conditions' of recognizability (Butler, 2009: 4), including juridico-political ones in ways that are different in part due to geopolitical power relations. We contend that the struggle for a liveable life is to be aware of the limitations of what is given. However, we do not finish there; we see that an awareness of such limitations enables articulation and recognition of something more that pushes those limitations to create what is possible.

In Chapter 5, we explore the possibilities of liveable lives. This flows from Chapter 4 where we contend that the key to liveabilities is the potential for lives to be liveable without proscribing how this might be obtained, as well as from Chapter 3, where we do not negate but complicate juridico-political frames. In this chapter, we describe how we created experimental spaces to consider and perform liveable lives through theatre workshops and street theatres through the *Liveable Lives* project. Conceptually, we move from ordinary to commonplace to further the contestations of inclusion/exclusion and suggest the place of the ordinary in 'the common', not to negate individual pursuits, but to explore collective 'commons'. Bringing this together with how we worked locally in and through the spaces of Brighton and Kolkata, the chapter seeks to engage space as the spatial-temporal contingencies of liveabilities. These locals are connected across geopolitical borders through liveabilities' performative aspects. This was not premised on universalizing the concept, which may then apply to persons across the globe; instead, whilst the method might be explored and deployed elsewhere, the particularities surrounding the theatre workshops and performances in Brighton and Kolkata were enabling and allowed for transnational conversations.

The conclusion offers a change of tone and focuses on the dialogue between the authors and those who worked with them as activisms on the project, Leela Bakshi and Sumita. The edited exchange undertaken in 2022 is framed around their responses to the book, the import of liveable lives and a concept and what this means in 2022 as the world moves through a global pandemic with intense and often unrecognized implications for the liveabilities of LGBTQ people.

Note for (social science?) readers

We wish to leave you with two points as we discuss our conceptualizations and fieldwork data. First, in each of the chapters, when we share excerpts from our different methodological sites interspersed with each other, we do so with the hope that they will allow the reader to undertake an interpretive journey of these conversations, excerpts and images; that they will read beyond our readings, developing their engagements, in ways that we cannot envisage. The quotes, narratives and collages that we select and share are juxtaposed to enable a critical reading practice that rejects comparison and embraces transnational dialogue. Second, when we share the excerpts, we purposely focus on the narration of the lived experience rather than the identity. This is because we want to focus on the social relations within which persons either marked or identifying as LGBTQ experience their bodies and selves. Because sexual and gender identities are geographically specific and used in juridico-political frames to distinguish between the forward and the backward, we take a bold step to use them to frame the project/this book and yet step away from specific categories of understanding individuals/lives. The conditions under which lived experience becomes tied to the knowledge of liveability are thus through the theorization/usage of the lived body by the narrators and their interpretation by the research teams, rather than the identities that participants used or did not use. Through this, liveability exists in this book as a concrete set of relations, and its narration of material lives co-constructing each other. As we move through this book, we use liveability as a conceptual term in ways that are grateful but not stuck to Butler's work on livability. Throughout the book, liveability travels and, then towards the end of the book, is performed and in the final chapter emerges as a collective conversation that engages differences across people and places that constructed this research and yet have journeyed since.

Concluding manoeuvres: Liveabilities through *Liveable Lives*

Liveable lives seeks to work in decolonial ways with the concept of liveability. It builds on Butler's consideration of a 'good life' to think about what makes a life, life for LGBTQ people in India and Great Britain. In doing so, it questions measures of liveability and asks instead for considerations of the possibilities of ordinariness and creating liveable lives as academic and political aims. As this book conceptualizes liveabilities through decolonial reflections and participants narratives, we offer the following entry points.

Firstly, that we reject juridico-political norms of recognizability can be assessed and compared through international/national/local metres of inclusion and exclusion, based on legislative and political standardized measures that reproduce colonial frames (Chapter 2). Such norms fail to understand the precarities of those recognized as humans residing in nations that do have rights, in addition to foreclosing an understanding of the nuanced and active agentic lives of queer bodies in countries without rights. It allows for an optic of liveability that includes figuring out ways to endure, persist and how to 'become possible' (Butler, 2004b: 31), where the 'good life' is denied as well as granted. Yet, throughout this book, we are careful not to draw a false equivalence around the struggle for liveability across populations that inhabit gaping geopolitical divides; differential precarities mean profoundly different forms of violence, lack of access to infrastructure, injuries, destructions, with many rooted in continuing colonial divides. We contend instead that *precisely because* life across geopolitical contexts is not equally precarious, despite a condition of precariousness affecting all, asking critical questions through an optic of liveability forces us to re-think uninterrogated socio-political contexts within which lives either become complacent or struggle to be viable. Liveability thus recognizes that even where lives are ostensibly precarious and may be viable in terms of a survivable life, they may also not be liveable (Chapters 3 and 4).

Secondly, our transnational engagement with the question of liveable lives via (non)normative lives will be understood around life events, historical moments and deeply affective states of the mind. As we go forward, we will explore how space, place and time intersected during the project workshops and interviews to understand liveability.

We will demonstrate that liveability does not exist in isolation but is an interdependent concept and practice. Even as one narrates and sorts one's memories, aspirations and thoughts, liveability emerges to grapple with and sometimes counter its own standardized and dominant form. Liveability is thus not an insular experience or phenomenon but deeply relational with a structure, one's self and others.

Thirdly, we will examine living *with* surviving, the normative and non-normative, the ordinary and the everyday, seeing all three as central to a liveable life related to conscious practices, material realities and aspirations of living. Each of these schemas uses fragments of conversations and excerpts from interviews and group discussions, as well as collages engaging with the narrator, instead of using them as raw data to make a point. The attempt is that the conceptual schemas will allow the reader to undertake an interpretive journey of these conversations, excerpts and images. The fragments delineated in these sites must be read contextually in contingent and historically specific ways. More importantly, the quotes, narratives and collages that we select and share are juxtaposed to enable a critical reading practice that rejects comparison and embraces a grounded dialogue.

Finally, we see hope in the potentials of liveabilities and the creation of other times/places, even momentarily, where collectively performing liveability becomes an act of liveability. We see desire, hope and striving for utopias, even where life becomes less survivable in this pursuit as key to engagements with liveabilities. It is not just where we are, but where we might be. It is not only what makes life liveable now, but also what might life (more) liveable in the future. The desire for a liveable lives might make life bearable now in the hope for more/better and the recognition that what we have is/may not be enough.

2

Liveability as a decolonial option through collaborative research and activisms

Introduction

This chapter opens discussions of liveability as a decolonial option through collaborative research and activisms. 'Liveability' offers a conceptual optic and a methodological direction to counter colonizing discourses of forward/backward nations and attendant material implications across sites of colonial difference and structural differentiation. Through this book, we share consideration of the lifeworlds of people who practise, express and identify with diverse sexualities and genders in their situatedness within the forward/backward mesh. In doing so, we join those voices that are involved in critiquing the different ways in which forward/backward temporalities define and are defined by questions of sexualities and genders and, in turn, contribute to the idea of freedom and progress (Butler, 2009; Kulpa & Silva, 2016; Puar, 2007; Rao, 2020). We formulate our critique by doing a decolonial reading of liveability. This reading then develops through an engagement with the following in our work:

(a) Research practices that are potential connectors of lives across sites of differential precarity and places of colonial difference.
(b) The ordinary lifeworlds within the everyday, which we use as temporal and conceptual markers. The everyday is the focus of Chapters 3 and 4 and developed through commons in Chapter 5, around queer lives and activisms that, despite

being juridically unintelligible, are folded into queerphobic and xenophobic renderings of nationalist discourses.

(c) Forms of living that, while juridically intelligible and normalized within liberal majoritarian politics, are struggling to be viable within complacent states (Chapter 3).

The stabilities of decolonial thought in Anglo-American academies are recently under critique for ignoring theorization from the Global South, including those works that do the work of decolonizing, even when not using the term 'decolonial' (Moosavi, 2020). We are not scholars of decolonial thought and a historical analysis in the Anglo-American academy and the Global South is beyond the scope of this chapter. From our vantage in queer and transnational studies, we deploy a decolonial lens. Queer studies turn to a decolonial lens to understand the 'inter-implications of gender and sexuality in coloniality' (Jivraj, Bakshi & Posocco, 2020: 454). Departing from single issue politics about gender-sexual rights, decolonial queer work interrogates the relations of power in colonial and postcolonial structures both *as* queer subjects and *alongside* historically oppressed communities. Not all such interrogations reach the academy because either they are part of the everyday life of critical activist collectives in various parts of the Global South or they do not use the English term 'decolonial' to mark their discourse. Its recent scholarly trajectory, therefore, should not be taken as a novelty, but as a much-needed intervention in queer studies to (a) talk about the ordering of gender(ed)-sexual(ized) lives with oppressive states, (b) hold space for academics and activists across southern and northern contexts[1] for collaborative work, and (c) to interrogate the operations of colonial logic in social, political and economic structures.

In countering nation-states' forward/backward narratives, we argue that liveability emerges as a decolonial option precisely because it holds the potential to engage with sexual(ized) lives that are not necessarily tied to legislation and equalities. Legislation and equalities are core to the conception of the liberal rights bearing subject and the autonomous individual, within which sexual autonomy is central. We do not argue against rights and autonomy but hold accountable claims to rights that follow an uninterrogated Eurocentric model.[2] The location of a 'non-Eurocentric' subject within our field of work is not our objective, as the link between the colony and the postcolony is much too deep, in both material and psychic ways. More importantly, we are interested in countering the legislative and equalities aspects of the Eurocentric model that holds forward/backward narratives together, marking places 'over here' as winning in contrast to the 'over there'. The here and there is typically associated with national boundaries of the Global North and Global South, which runs through the many iterations in global discourses of sexual rights and development and aid. While it is this that we counter in this book, the 'here and there'/'north and south' are also placeholders such that even within the same national boundary, there will be geographical imaginings played out as comparisons that name cultures and regions as forward/backward.

In what follows, we delineate our (the authors) locations and read the figure of the 'Indian Queer' and the 'British Queer' with the lens of coloniality. After that, we expand on the specificities of collaborative research and activist collaborations that created this research, which elaborates upon the transnational methodological insights from Chapter 1. Furthering the forward/backward narrative from the introductory chapter, we then follow up with a critical reading of geographical imaginings of the UK/India that seek to reiterate here/there in national and local contexts. We arrive at liveability as a decolonial option through these above routes and conclude with some key observations that we take through the book.

Ourselves

Before we move ahead, we pause to provide some locational and contextual notes about ourselves, as authors and people. There are debates within feminist traditions, specifically feminist geographies, regarding positionality and its relation to place, importance, and narcissism (see Domosh, 2003; Vanderbeck, 2005). We see their value less in the 'revelation' of 'who we are' as defined by a list of identities and more in how the construction of this project and this book relied on 'us', was created through us, and the power relations that form us. This is important to show how sexualized/gendered colonial power relations reconstitute liveable lives.

Niharika

Queer, সমকামী (*samakamee*/desiring the same) colonial subjects such as myself are making their liveabilities *within* and *through* much contested binaries of modernity/tradition, civilized/uncivilized and forward/backward. I have lived my personal, professional and activist life across India and the United States. My place of *dwelling* shaped me more than my place of actual residence.[3] Therefore, in the United States, I dwelled as a 'queer woman of colour', with some class privileges in the Weberian sense. In India, I dwell as a 'queer woman', সমকামী নারী (*samakamee naree*/woman who desires the same), carrying privileges and protections of caste and class. Across both contexts, I carried and still carry cis-privileges, but not in an absolute way and with different histories. I self-identify as a 'queer academic-activist', as সমকামী নারী (*samakamee naree*/woman who desires the same) in this present historical moment. The classificatory terms that I use to introduce myself are not ontological categories but what Walter Mignolo would term as 'enactment of classification' that, while assumed to be based on ontological categories, are fictional classifications dependent on local histories (2016: ix). At the time of writing this book (which took up the majority of the 2021 calendar year), I have been managing the effects of the pandemic-induced lockdown with my queer kins, caring for those I love through distance and proximity, trying to create calm with/in routine institutional edicts and behaviour that make neurodivergent workers like me feel disturbingly devalued and dysfunctional. The University College Dublin fellowship had helped create some precious time and headspace to begin work on this book on a remote basis, even when I was continuing to handle institutional demands and the care and loss of those proximal and far. These strains of un/liveability underlie the writing of this book.

Kath

Perhaps I occupy a neo-liberalized assimilated subject position yet still marginal to centre as a lesbian, tenured, white person with significant Anglo-American privilege. I have lived most of my professional and adult life in the UK. I am Irish by birth and identity. I dwelled seemingly seamlessly in England, in 'Gay Brighton' for thirteen years until May 2016. The Brexit referendum, to my mind, named many of us Irish/migrants who dwelled with racial privilege as unwelcome foreigners. I now live in Ireland, still marked by my privilege but much more visibly marked as 'the Lesbian' in my personal and professional life, 'the Lesbian' in the department, 'the Lesbian' mother and 'the Lesbian' neighbour. Until I became single, this marking was often seen as acceptable copy of the heteronormative family, 'like us', but not like us simultaneously. As a single lesbian mother, I am less easily placed and I notice more discomfort in others. The Marriage referendum that enabled same-sex marriage in Ireland in 2015 marked a legally accepted/acceptable same sex relationship in and through the 'New Ireland'. As I make less sense in the heteronormative worlds I inhabit, I still retain other privileges that cushion this lack of recognition.

The geographies, as well as the histories, create fictional categories that have material and affective manifestations. Writing this book during Covid, remotely with Niharika, over various zoom meetings, was undertaken for me during periods of lockdown, which meant homeschooling, work pressures and other life challenges, including relationship ending/reforming. Whilst I have secure housing, neurotypical children, stable employment and finances, I felt the strains on my life as liveable. Losing face-to-face connections with people made some moments, days and weeks feel bearable but not a life that is a life. Writing a book such as this remotely also made it more functional, in contrast to the passion and life that was the project. We felt it needed to be written to honour those who told us their stories and speak beyond the legislative and colonial hierarchies discussed in this chapter. Yet, as with the project itself, revisiting those moments of connection, joy and pain also created moments of liveability, as the project did (see Banerjea et al., 2016).

Coloniality and the figure of the 'Indian Queer' and 'British Queer'

Academic writings on decoloniality, including its feminist renderings, argue that the power characterizing the logic of modernity is coloniality or the colonial matrix of power. The colonial matrix of power is an assemblage of various relations of power, including gender, sexuality, race, capitalism (Bacchetta, 2016; Lugones, 2010) and caste. These relations, while characterizing colonialism, are extended into current discourses and practices (Bacchetta, 2016). The term 'coloniality', when juxtaposed with modernity, works to name 'a narrative that builds Western civilisation by celebrating its achievements while hiding at the same time its darker side …'; in other words, 'there is no modernity without coloniality' (Mignolo, 2011a: 2). Coloniality does not stop with political independence from colonizers, but crucially remains as a 'socio-epistemic formation' that organizes knowledge and experience (Posocco, 2016: 250). For the colonial subject, accounting for oneself is, therefore, 'an impossibility' but also 'imperative' (Posocco, 2016: 250), as categorizations are inadequate but also necessary. A decolonial stance then requires a different account of oneself; while still attached to colonizing epistemes, it makes a critical attempt to de-link itself from that episteme and present alternatives, if not entirely new lenses of accounting for oneself. When deployed to critique hegemonic discourses around genders and sexualities, decolonial work goes beyond the 'simple inclusion of those on the "academic peripheries"' and 'rebuilding of epistemological foundations' of contemporary research practices (Kulpa & Silva, 2016: 140–1). To this end, a decolonial take allows us to re-signify a field that is 'already marked by the coloniality of power' (Bakshi, Jivraj & Posocco, 2016: 6–7). It is this task of re-signification that we put liveability to. Liveability is useful to critically look at globalizing discourses of forward/backward orders – wherever they exist. The term has helped us disturb the normalizing discourse of sexual progress within colonial renderings of sexuality rights, as they are tied to only legislation and equalities.

The figure of the 'Indian queer'

The diverse forms of gender-sexual practices, expressions and identities in India inhabit a spatio-temporal bind, in 'the in-betweens' (Ekine, 2016) of the British empires' 'epistemic weapons' (Mignolo, 2016) and contextual heteropatriarchies that are imbricated with the colonial, rational time of nation, family and community. Within the Indian cultural context, the 'homosexual', the 'single woman', the 'unmarried woman', the 'Muslim man', the 'tribal woman', the 'Scheduled Caste'[4] are figures that hold within them colonial and postcolonial histories, most often violent, that are constitutive of the univocal ordering of capital and time in our cultures. Differentially abject figures are constitutive of the ideal Hindu, heterosexual, homosocial, upper-caste, middle-class citizen-subject. Therefore, the homosexual figure, while not legally recognized until 6 September 2018,[5] but even after that, is intrinsic to the linear ordering of the Hindu imagination, discourses of nationalism and the ideal citizen-subject. In discussing the significance of queer genders and sexualities to postcolonial right-wing Hindu nationalism, Paola Bacchetta argues that both 'queerphobia' and 'queerphilia' are 'integral to the formation, maintenance, and deployment of Hindu nationalism' (2013: 122). Within discourses of Hindu nationalism, queerphobia does not necessarily present itself in isolation but reworks colonial sexual and gender normativities and presents itself with xenophobia. This occurs in two ways. As Bacchetta explains, 'xenophobic queerphobia' operates by 'constructing the self-identified Indian queer as originating outside the nation', and 'queerphobic xenophobia' works by assigning queer genders and sexualities 'to all the designated Others of the nation regardless of their sexual conduct or identity' (Bacchetta, 2013: 123). Now, the Hindu imagination does contain not only queerphobia but also queerphilia. When Hindu religious symbolism is drawn upon to present a hyper-valorized queer, what we have is 'queerphilic idealisation' (Bacchetta, 2013: 122). We can often see this in discourses that attempt to represent queer genders and sexualities as authentic subjects of the Indian nation by excavating them from Hindu epics and religious texts. This is the context within which queers in India reside, with several involved in various activisms, some intricately aligned with feminist collectives and movements.

The figure of the 'British Queer'

The figure British Queer once maligned and denied full citizenship through a heteropatriarchal state (Bell & Binnie, 2000) has apparently 'won' in state legislative policy and accepted culturally (Weeks, 2007). Employment, marriage and protections for goods and services mark the British queer as 'lucky', 'leading the way' and exceptional compared to other less liberal regimes and contexts. The hierarchization of the British Queer is noted in 'Rainbow indexes' and other moments of national comparisons, reiterating a superiority that mirrors colonial engagements with 'civilization' as well as the vilification and othering of 'other places'. This marking has specific effects, creating the British queer through naming less progressive others (see Browne & Banerjea et al., 2015; Lalor & Browne, 2018).

The geopolitical reconstruction of Britishness in and through the queer (or more accurately specific figures of usually gay men, arguably not queer at all within homonormative frames of reference) serves to mark Britishness as superior, through various 'rainbow' scales and indexes that note changes to and advances in juridico-political equalities. Same-sex marriage and the monogamous couple retain a centrality in the acceptable face of British Queerness, as well as through the implementation of equalities legislation (see Browne et al., 2016, chapter 3). The British colonial production of elsewhere, alongside ongoing geopolitical power relations, often remains unaccounted for, save for acknowledging colonial laws around sodomy, which are seen as 'in the past' for Britain, again placing other nations as 'backward' or not progressing/civilizing in this way. The figure of the British Queer then becomes one that 'saves' other queers from their (brown) oppressors, their lives unencumbered by marginalization or exclusion. Indeed, when they are, through issues such as 'hate crime', they remain 'lucky' to be part of the British national project, which seemingly emphasizes inclusion for 'all'. As discussed later in the chapter, this geographical imagining of the British Queer has specific effects on the 'here' and projections of othering on 'there'.

Collaborative research

Making Liveable Lives: Rethinking Social Exclusion asked, 'what makes liveable for LGBTQ persons across India and the UK?' As discussed in the introduction, we deliberately refuted comparative frames and methodologies that would hierarchize LGBTQ lives in the UK and India within the framings of the British/Indian Queer and the associated assumptions of lived experiences. Comparative methodologies have been part of colonial systems where 'the observer' remains 'uncontaminated' and privileges 'Western epistemology' over others (Mignolo, 2011a, 208). Juridico-political frames around queer lives typically compare the social health of populations and nations with a meter of the presence or absence of legal rights. This, we have argued (Browne & Banerjea et al., 2015), is likely to further progress/backwardness and modern/traditional binaries by classifying nation-states and populations along hierarchical lines. Deploying liveability outside a comparative frame allows us to move beyond familiar 'workings of neo-colonial epistemic categories, systems of classification and taxonomies that classify people' (Bakshi, Jivraj & Posocco, 2016: 1).

Theorizing together across the south and north through a liveability optic

We sought to actualize the contestations of comparative work by working collaboratively from a transnational methodological position across our sites of geopolitical divides and colonial difference (Browne, Banerjea et al., 2017). We are reconfiguring epistemological foundations of researching sexualities by not simply adding those from the Global South but theorizing across the south and north together through an optic of liveability. Our collaborative theoretical claim is based on liveability's decolonial potential as in part lying in its possibility to focus on the lives of those otherwise juridically unintelligible and folded into queerphobic and xenophobic renderings of nationalist discourses. At the same time, in places where juridical recognition is seemingly guaranteed, liveability facilitates a discussion about the forms of living that are also constitutive of such recognition, and hence inside-outside the realms of legal rationality. Perhaps even more radically, it also allows us to explore forms of living even where lives are otherwise juridically incomprehensible and research experiences that fail to reach the ideal of 'British Queer' for those whose lives *should be* recognized. Thus, throughout *Liveable Lives*, we discuss how LGBTQ persons across places of colonial difference create and introduce liveabilities in the cracks and fissures of hegemonic gender-sexual practices and normative regimes.

Until 6 September 2018, India, a former colony of the British empire, was legally burdened with Section 377 of the Indian Penal Code (hereafter referred to as S 377). Under the theme, 'Unnatural offences', S 377 states:

> Whoever voluntarily has carnal intercourse against the order of nature with any man, woman or animal, shall be punished with 1[imprisonment for life], or with imprisonment of either description for a term which may extend to ten years, and shall also be liable to fine. Explanation. – Penetration is sufficient to constitute the carnal intercourse necessary to the offence described in this section.

S 377 has its origins in an 1860 British colonial law. This imperial epistemic configuration prioritizes a singular understanding and posits itself as the only valid universal to understand sexual desire and behaviour. By rationally ordering and regulating the multiplicities of sexual behaviour, it has been part of racial classifications that underlie conceptions of the natural and unnatural. S 377 is not just a relic of colonial difference but has been a living epistemic reality that marks sexual behaviour outside of peno-vaginal acts as unnatural and therefore contained. As we noted in the introduction, it was read down by the Delhi High Court in the Naz Foundation vs Government of NCT of Delhi case on 2 July 2009, thereby decriminalizing consensual sexual acts outside of peno-vaginal ones.[6] On 11 December 2013, in the Suresh Kumar Kaushal vs Naz Foundation, the Supreme Court overturned the HC's decision after finding it 'legally unsustainable'.[7] This is the same year that the same-sex Marriage Act was passed in England and Wales, offering the British queer the apparent pinnacle of sexual rights and state recognition.[8]

On 6 September 2018, in the Navtej Singh Johar and Others vs Union of India case, the Supreme Court stated, 'S 377 is arbitrary ...' and 'majoritarian views and popular morality cannot dictate constitutional rights'.[9] Moving between this turmoil, S 377 all through is an obstinate colonial wound that is part of contemporary 'imperial classifications' (Mignolo, 2011a, location 612) and deployed to rank order and classify people and nation-states. While regulating and persecuting sexual behaviour that falls outside of peno-vaginal acts, S 377 has been consistently used to generate knowledge about queer lives and mark entire nations as homophobic, thus completely disqualifying forms of thinking and doing that is part of the 'body-politics'[10] of that place.[11]

As perceived champions of progress, social actors in the Global North, juxtaposing laws such as S 377 and the English and Welsh Marriage Act, use a comparative frame to address homophobia and social acceptance issues. Legislation emerges as a critical form of evidence in metrics and comparisons (Browne, Banerjea et al., 2015).

So, for instance, while the UK is generally seen as inclusive in terms of LGBTQ equalities and legislation, India was rated poorly in metrics of LGBTQ equalities during the period under study. Decriminalization and subsequent recriminalization have been used to describe it as one of the 'most homophobic countries' ahead of countries where homosexuality remains punishable by death (Batchelor, 2017; Nunez, 2017; Strasser, 2014). We sought to challenge some of the conclusions that we might draw from a focus on inclusive/exclusive legislation that places sexual and gender politics 'over there' (in India and often by extension the Global South) where we are 'losing', and frames 'us here' (in the UK, and often the Global North) as 'sorted' and 'winning'.

Therefore, we are making a call to move beyond the inclusive/exclusive legislative frame, as it is part of a more extensive colonial sexual rhetoric and its reworked forms. This sexual rhetoric, as Sabsay argues, operates as 'a marker' to distinguish 'the so-called advanced western democracies in opposition to their "undeveloped others"', thereby justifying 'the current re-articulation of orientalist and colonial politics' (2012: 606). The inclusive/exclusive legislative binary has the effect of racializing 'regions and areas of the world' (Mignolo, 2016: xi). It has geographical manifestations and imaginaries, most prominently in the differentiation of the Global North as 'progressive' and the Global South as 'backwards' (Kupla & Mizielińska, 2011; Kulpa & Silva, 2016; Rao, 2014, 2020; Silva & Ornat, 2016). The dualism may (a) legally address forms of queerphobic xenophobia and xenophobic queerphobia and (b) influence nation-states to reset exclusionary legislations. But it does not go far enough in fracturing universalized and nationalist temporalities that are part of colonial power and being. It conceals 'the irreducible cultural, political and economic dependencies in the inter-state system and, therefore, between nation and nationalities' (Mignolo, 2016: xv).

This hierarchization has material implications for development politics (Banerjea & Browne, 2018; Browne & Banerjea et al., 2015).

The superiority of the Global North concerning sexual rights can invoke and has been invoked as a rationale for moral authority and, at times, military intervention (see, for example, Currah, 2013; Hubbard & Wilkinson, 2015; Morgensen, 2010; Oswin, 2007; Puar, 2007, 2013). Coupled with this, allocation of monetary funding has begun to be linked (uneasily) to LGBTQ rights. In 2018, the Danish government withheld aid to Tanzania because of homophobic comments by Tanzania officials (Adebayo & Kottasova, 2018). This follows the withdrawal of assistance from Uganda earlier this decade after Uganda's Anti-Homosexuality Bill was signed by President Yoweri Museveni. Norway and Denmark cut their aid support (Plaut, 2014). The decision reiterated the UK's position of channelling support away from the government through alternative routes for the Ugandan people (see Rao, 2014). While debating how to mainstream LGBTQ rights in its development agendas (Tyson, 2014), the World Bank has drafted an economic assessment report for homophobia in India (Badgett, 2014). Similarly, the European Parliament had voted to include LGBTQ rights in its development policies (European Parliament Intergroup on LGBT Rights, 2014). Hence, the place of LGBTQ rights in a (supra-)nation's plan and its link to economic growth and development aid is not an innocent progressive indicator of change that addresses global homophobia; instead, it creates and reiterates, and does not simply reflect, a colonial matrix of power.

Further, when considered against the background of the Indian nationalist articulations of queerphobia and xenophobia and queerphilia and the British understandings of superiority in terms of sexual rights, the inclusion/exclusion legislative frame also functions to mark oppositions between the 'traditional here' and the 'modern there', that can never be subsumed within the imaginaries of the national body and/or its nationalist aspirations. This is colonial politics with both its assimilationist liberal and right-wing versions that are part of more extensive processes of marginalizations, dispossessions and structural differentiations that emerge from interconnected processes of militarization and incarceration within ever-increasing fundamentalist and hyper-nationalist regimes. The power differentials which are otherwise hidden between comparisons of legal reforms for the queer figure can be made visible through interrogating and ultimately moving beyond the inclusion/exclusion dualism.

Moving beyond this dualism recognizes that inclusion/exclusion legislative parameters cannot capture lives and forms of living that reside within and outside of juridico-political frames of intelligibility. While such binaries are based on an attempted process of rational enumeration of the pre/absence of legal rights, lives and forms of living that escape and/or exceed such enumeration become silenced or obscured. Moving towards an exploration of what makes life liveable for LGBTQ people enables us to grapple theoretically with this fundamental colonial temporal-geographical logic as present within queerphobia and xenophobia and sexual and gendered progress/backwardness narratives. Thus, we set out to empirically situate/locate/develop liveabilities of LGBTQ persons across the UK and India to understand our contextual vulnerabilities, interdependencies and material realities of individual and collective belongings.

Transnational as a methodology to contest colonial comparisons

We used a transnational methodological entry point to operationalize our research and, in doing so, to open the potential of exploring liveabilities in ways that question coloniality inherent to academic thinking and methodological practice. We deploy transnational to mean dialoguing and creating knowledge from our places of colonial difference without seeking sameness. As explained in the introduction, our entire methodological endeavour has been to jointly develop our research, including a research design that shared questions but implemented differently. Our mix of project workshops, in-depth unstructured interviews, online questionnaires and street theatre took shape through context and the networks and relations. We thus rerouted ourselves through the local even as we were working within the transnational. This allowed us to move away from 'methodological normativities' that typically considers places as static units of analysis, from which comparisons are made in terms of dualisms, such as degrees of 'freedom' and 'unfreedom' (Browne & Banerjea et al., 2017).

A research practice based on a transnational methodology with liveability as an epistemic category allowed us to focus on the social patterning of experiences that reside outside and yet within colonial and nationalist logics. Hinging on distinctions between modern and traditional, modern and non-modern, backward and forward, such logic attempts to regulate by denying or challenging the existence of worlds with different ontological premises. Such denial and challenge are the workings of colonial power. A focus on liveability has the potential to open the way (or indeed multiple ways) to more transformative discourses by putting into circulation conceptual tools to decolonize 'general historical schema or schemas that establish domains of the knowable' (Butler, 2009: 6–7). Liveability, methodologically operationalized through our transnational entry point, offered us opportunities to empirically explore the unease felt by many in the UK regarding the supposed completion of LGBTQ equalities agendas with the passing of same-sex marriage and other legislation, and the also problematic assumptions of backwardness associated with India following the reinstatement of S 377 of the Indian Penal Code.

Activist collaborations

Collaboration with activists is central to our work and how we imagine liveability as part of our academic-activist critique. It is a way to re-link with ways of *doing and thinking*, with patterns of 're-existence' (Mignolo, 2011a: location 677)[12] that are otherwise hidden or objectified within the troubled separation of academia from activism. Therefore, collaboration with activists is part of our 'epistemic disobedience' (Mignolo, 2011b: 3)[13] that refuses to produce knowledge within exclusive walls of the academy.

Feminist, queer-feminist, and decolonial writers, scholars and activists remind us of the usefulness and political implications of collaboration with activists in research, as well as their limitations and inherent power relations. Locations, politics and histories often get hidden within the process of academic knowledge production; thus, it is important to note where, how, why and by who knowledge is produced (Haraway, 1988; Harding, 1998; Monk & Hanson, 1982; Rose, 1993; Silva & Ornat, 2016; Stanley & Wise, 1983). This sensibility runs through *Liveable Lives* and specifically the transnational co-production with activists across the UK and India.[14] The main collaborators included, in Brighton, England, Leela Bakshi (Independent Activist Researcher) and Nick McGlynn (Research Assistant), and in Kolkata, India, Sumita Beethi and Dr. Ranjita Biswas (research team), and Rukmini Banerjee (Research Associate). The latter are members of Sappho for Equality who were interested in the question of liveabilities.[15] Our research teams, therefore, constituted members across activist and academic sites. These people however were not unknown to us and occupied various positionings and relationships with us. They were and are friends, lovers and daughter. These relationalities did not preclude the process of research, which from the start was never imagined through the oft-critiqued researcher-researched binary. They allowed a research experiment to unfold where relationships were nurtured because of shared (but also fractured) visions of the social. In fact, these relationships and friendships were also brought into re-existence 'through the construction of an ethics' concerning research and writing together (Banerjea, Dasgupta et al., 2018: 5). At the same time, as a team comprising both academics and activists, in their professional and personal roles we acknowledge 'the continuing relations of power that are manifest in and through these relationships' (Browne & Banerjea et al., 2017: 5).

Even though the activists were meaningfully involved during the writing phase, they also, understandably, declined to get extensively involved in academic writing, notably academic papers (and this book). They had limited time and sought other avenues for activism. Yet they contributed to opening conversations and discussions during the project regarding what should be written, which arguments were crucial, and how these could be framed. When it neared completion, they returned to academic writing, giving them the author's status for any publications they wished to contribute to. Articles and outputs were co-drafted and written between the academics on the project, so transnationally created and curated in ways that made sense for us all. From within our places of colonial difference, we were literally thinking ourselves out 'through collective practice and particular kinds of theorising' (Alexander & Mohanty, 1997). The activists who collaborated with us did so because they are interested in creating and consolidating collective social systems that will enable and facilitate queer loves and ways of living, and not in an isolated way, critically connected to other forms of dispossessions. Seeing academic and activist work as helpful in this endeavour, it was also clear that there are limits to the use of academic writing by these activists compared to the energy expended; so, this book is written by the academics who felt both a responsibility to honour and develop this thinking in service of both activists and scholars and recognized the place of this form of writing in their paid employment. Yet, we conclude the book with an afterword with words from Leela and Sumita, to reflect on responses and considerations beyond the academics that wrote *Liveable Lives*.

Despite these differing roles, the conceptualizations of liveabilities were informed by and informed the activists' work. For example, the term 'liveability', with its Bengali transliterations such as জীবনের মতো জীবন (*jeeboner mato jeebon*/a life that is like a life), বেঁচে থাকা (*benche thaka*/to live), ভাল থাকা (*bhalo thaka*/staying well), for a while was part of SFE's advocacy and awareness efforts, along with terms such as 'discrimination' / বৈষম্য (*boishamya*) and 'rights' / অধিকার (*adhikar*) that the organization uses. Research work, a part of SFE's funded endeavours, is crucial for its vision of socially transformative politics; the organization has been researching and documenting different aspects of the lives of lesbian, bisexual identifying and transmasculine persons to understand structures of normative violence and discrimination across social institutions. These efforts at social transformation bear more significance in the light of the fact that S 377 never directly named or implicated lesbian lives. The letter of the law addressed only carnal intercourse against the order of nature where penile penetration is a necessary condition to constitute the offence and for all practical purposes indicates sodomy. On the one hand, this judicial invisibility offered some level of protection to lesbian and bisexual identifying women; on the other hand, lesbian expressions remain an invisibilized spot in the Indian heteropatriarchal state machinery, which refuses to acknowledge the fact that 'women' *do* love 'women' and cohabit with them. Given this context, SFE's advocacy and activism have aimed to break socio-cultural and emotional-intellectual barriers and build spaces for difference and celebration. While legal reform has been a pillar of the struggle for equality and non-discrimination, Sappho for Equality has taken its work beyond to engage students, teachers, law enforcement officials, doctors, grassroots workers in the development sector to talk about violence, discrimination and support systems.

Given that the scope of the law as an agent of emancipation is limited and that lesbian, bisexual and transmasculine lives are lived through multifarious forms of violation, there is a need to have different terms to 'break the silence'. 'Breaking the silence' involves the process of identification and articulation of marginalization and invisibilization, albeit in terms that can be communicated. While admitting that there are some silences, some sufferings that cannot be articulated in language and can only be grasped at the perceptual level, it is nevertheless vital to be able to find a language to communicate that can then become a possible path to address such hitherto unacknowledged pain and seek justice thereof. Sappho for Equality's queer feminist politics is situated in this space of heterogeneity and multiple possibilities, in which the concept of liveability and its Bangla transliterations such as জীবনের মতো জীবন (*jeeboner mato jeebon*/a life that is like a life), বেঁচে থাকা (*benche thaka*/to live) and ভাল থাকা (*bhalo thaka*/staying well) acquires significance.

For at least four reasons, collaboration with activists can bring about a more critical imagination of liveability. Firstly, as we alluded to earlier, the concept of liveability allows us to think beyond legal reform and diminish our over-dependence on the symbolic excess that such reforms bring. Working with activists foregrounds the lived experiences and politically grounded realities of these conceptual interrogations. Second, imagining a 'better future' from within our locations and beyond them is much of what animates the decolonial rendering of liveability. Collaboration with activists can illuminate how everyday activisms that go into the making of collective histories generate diverse imaginations of liveabilities that, while actively supporting legal reforms, are not limited to reformist agendas. For instance, queer feminists in India are engaged in strategically broadening the discussion around family and kinship to include considerations of relationalities (concerning inheritance, succession, visitation, adoption, etc.) outside of blood and marriage ties. Further, activists who live with and through unrecognized or stigmatized desires have a unique vantage to theorize the actualities of power relations that circumscribe making a liveable life. This theorization often includes imagination of liveable futures that are also ethical. While drawing from existing norms and institutional structures, such imaginations also strive to give a different account of one's relations with these institutions. Thus, activist collaborations, especially in contexts that are still waiting for legal reforms or do not entirely depend on them, can show possibilities to reconfigure colonial relations of power. The forward/backward dualism that undergirds the hierarchization of nation-states in terms of sexuality/gendered politics can have the effect of erasing such everyday activist efforts and collective histories that generate these imaginations. If we read sexualities only through the juridico-political lens, then legal equalities reforms, and by default, the Global North, become the primary placeholders to produce queer liveabilities, in comparison to a 'cultural imaginary' of places in the Global South as lacking such liveabilities or waiting for only legal reforms as the sole enabler of a liveable life. Developing this thinking further through empirics in Chapter 4, we ground the possibilities of liveable lives as a decolonial consideration of LGBTQ identifying lives, hopes and possibilities.

Having argued for activist collaborations, we are not indicating that activist sites are clear of hierarchies, inequitable power relations or stand outside the privileges and marginalizations of broader societies. In this project, we did not interrogate marginalizations and hierarchies of difference around race, caste, location, (dis)ability and religion concerning our working together or working within discussions of sexualities and genders in activist workings. Working across nations, considering decolonial power relations and working with LGBTQ as th primary unit of our analyses were important and relevant for the activists we created the research with. It was also imperfect, power laden in terms of UK funding and deadlines that made specific power structures and responsibilities for reporting. When discussing race/caste, we found that there are silences, othering as we look on one way and not another (for an expanded discussion, see Browne & Banerjea et al., 2017). In prioritizing sexualities and gender as a mode through which to view liveabilities, there is work to do to augment these discussions, including through intersectional/racialized lens and engagements with multiple marginalizations within and beyond research teams. We do not undertake this work here but name these complexities as crucial for operationalizing a decolonial frame that explores liveabilities. Here, we recognize that in arguing for activist collaborations for a better imagination of liveable lives, we contend that our theorizations of liveabilities need to be situated within activist histories that are struggling (and associated power relations) to *make lives liveable* beyond sexual and gender legal reforms. This 'making' includes advocacy and awareness, and research that is partial, situated and imperfect. In other words, activism happens through research collaborations that feed into advocacy and awareness efforts; yet, there is always more to be done.

Better than elsewhere? Geographical imaginings of 'other places'

As discussed in the Introduction, we conceptualize liveability through Judith Butler's thinking around 'what makes a life liveable' (2004a, 2004b). We introduced thinking through liveability on the terrain of LGBTQ lives, which brings everyday and often ordinary lifeworlds, otherwise hidden or left unexamined within juridico-political renderings of queer lives and activisms. We finish this chapter by exploring the macro-geographical imaginings to situate our considerations of liveabilities through a decolonial lens. Liveability as a concept can work as a connector of lives across sites of differential precarity and places of colonial difference. Consequently, using liveability, we avoid placing nations and, by implication, lives, in neat narratives of progress and backwardness, that a juridico-political lens serves to further. It is well recognized that there is a problem with an overdependence on legal reforms as being able to encompass and solve all forms of inequalities in society, including around sexual and gender differences (Binnie, 2004; Duggan, 2002; Stychin, 2003). A lens of liveability allows us to challenge this 'symbolic overload' (Garcia, 2016: 234). We cannot take the promise of legal reforms for granted, as only some are privileged enough to have access to it. Also, as this book argues, legal reforms are consequential to dominant narratives of colonial difference, including of here/there, forward/backward. Turning to participants' readings of sexual geopolitics, we ground these theoretical moves in their understandings to place them in conversation.

We found that engagements with juridico-political regimes are grounded in geographically imaginaries of progress that resulted in 'here/there'. It has long been argued that the self and 'here' is formed in part through reading distant 'there' and 'foreign' others (Said, 1978), and such geographical imaginaries have been key to conceptualizations of everyday geographies of sexualities, including East/West (Kulpa & Mislineski, 2011), and the urban/rural divide (Brown & Browne, 2016; McGlynn, 2018). Silva and Ornat (2016) point to the Global North/Global South divide as a critical mechanism through which geographies of sexualities are reproduced epistemologically. In our work, participants recreated Global North/Global South dichotomies, seeing entire continents as unsafe, reflecting the 'dangerous' and 'dark' continents, this time through a sexual and gendered lens that focuses on legislation and media coverage about the pre/absence of legislative reforms:

Can you think of a place that makes you feel that as an LGBTQ person, your life is or may not be liveable there?
- India is pretty high on the list, as is the middle east, many parts of Africa, large swathes of south east Asia
  (Online survey response)
- Africa
  (Online survey response)

These geographical imaginings create a dangerous other there, where whole continents are rendered as places where LGBTQ lives are not given the possibility of being liveable. Places are equated (India, Middle East, Africa, South-East Asia) and considered 'high on the list'. The list refers to numerous other countries where life is or may not be liveable. In contrast to the vast otherness of places that are considered not liveable, the liveability of 'here' is presumed as always better:

> **As an LGBT person, what makes your life not liveable?**
> Not much when I consider the hurt and pain that LGBTs undergo on a daily basis in other countries.
> (Online questionnaire response)

The hurt and pain of others' daily lives 'elsewhere' seemingly overshadow any potential contestations of liveability 'here'. The discourse becomes comparative, 'I am fine because they are not'. This construction of 'here' as 'fine' and 'there' as 'not fine' repeatedly emerged in project workshops and at various scales. Feeding into and from the figure of the British Queer and its other elsewhere, some British participants coded maps given in project workshops by identifying certain places (neighbourhoods, regions, countries, continents) as 'dangerous', 'not LGBTQ friendly' or 'not liveable'. Whilst local and national maps were often read through travels, migrations and life histories, world maps were reproduced often through specific geopolitical frames. Franco's map (see Figure 3) reiterates a particular spatial location of liveable/non-liveable/bearable. He narrated it by saying:

> Italy is where I'm from and that is definitely bearable but there still is a lot of homophobia and it's a very Catholic country which unfortunately does affect that. So life is definitely bearable but if I have to compare it to the UK, it's definitely not as advanced in terms of gay laws … Russia, as everyone will know, they are a very

anti-gay country. Most of Asia just with a question mark because I don't know so much about those countries ... I think South American in general is more bearable than liveable ... I don't think there is as much hate as there is for example in Africa, but I think it's not necessarily accepted like it is in other countries like England.

(Project Workshop, UK)

In Franco's narrative, his distinctions between liveable/not liveable/bearable are read through specific juridico-legal frameworks that are seen as creating lives across the globe. Directly attributing liveabilities to these continents draws on his own experiences within Italy/England to create complex imaginings of inclusions/law/cultures/experiences where Italy and Eastern Europe become 'bearable'. England, for Franco, is one of the pinnacles where LGBTQ lives are accepted, and Africa is where hate is located.

These readings of the spatialities of hate were further complicated later in his interview, in which Franco related experiences of public homophobic abuse in the UK (these and other experiences are discussed in Chapter 3). Thus, geographical imaginings of here/there

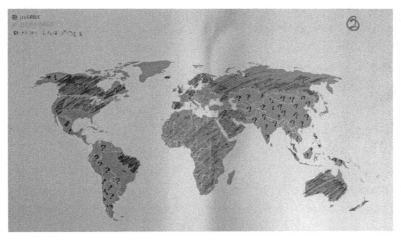

Figure 3 Franco's map created in Project Workshop.[16] Image: Author's own.

that are complicated through experiences are not seen to negate these readings. Instead, England remains 'accepting' and 'better than other places' through the presumptions of juridico-political acceptances leading to liveable lives. This understanding is replicated in LGBTQ events in the UK and elsewhere, where names of 'other places' are often carried as a mark of solidarity for those who do not have what it is supposed all LGBTQ people in the UK have in juridico-political terms (see also Lalor & Browne, 2018). In Brighton Pride in 2016, names of 'other places' where homosexuality remained illegal were used to 'politicize' the parade, which was increasingly being critiqued as apolitical and commercial (despite the involvement of local LGBT community groups and organizations who used the parade for visibility, feelings of inclusion and other political ends; see Browne & Bakshi, 2013).

Decolonial readings of that mark and name places as 'homophobic', hateful or liveable, speak more to the self, the here, rather than the places marked as other. In creating a politics that only references 'elsewhere', LGBTQ politics becomes synonymous with pointing out legislation and state-sponsored violence in other places, negating how liveabilities are contested here. If everything is 'sorted' here, for some gay men and lesbians, then there are no problems to be addressed by us all. The assumption of the panacea of legislative equalities means that battles here are 'won', and the uniting feature becomes 'our' support for 'them' elsewhere. Sexual politics then becomes displaced elsewhere. Thus, ongoing discriminations and marginalizations are to be ignored in favour of those 'poor others' in 'other places' that are imagined as not liveable.

The focus of this section so far, perhaps obviously, has been on sharing from UK respondents, in a place where the figure of the British Queer presumes acceptance and inclusion through LGBTQ equalities read as being achieved. In the India Media analysis, many news items and commentary in the wake of the 2013 decision to recriminalize same-sex activity were highly dismissive of the judgement as inconsistent and a 'step backwards'. This indicates that narratives of progress can operate within and between nations, where juridical changes such as these are read as moving 'back' to a past, in contrast to a more liberating/modern present. Interestingly, the narrative of progress and backwardness articulated through the here/there binary may not again necessarily be deployed within places with legislation but may also be used to differentiate between rural/urban divides in places without legislation. For instance, in the Indian context, there was a similar move to see the rural as 'elsewhere' as 'worse' than 'here', the urban:

> Suparna: I think it's because we are in a city we can live like this. In the film,[17] it was a village and obviously there was not enough awareness and education because of which there was so much problem.
>
> (Project Workshop, India)

There are problems with basing politics on 'other places' and 'other people', who need help and work and 'us' who are educated and 'can live like this'. Not only can it obscure and downplay sexual and gendered politics *here*, but when ongoing issues for LGBTQ people and concerns around particular normativities are no longer seen to be valid, the 'problem' becomes the person or the culture *with a* problem. This can further marginalize and exclude those already marginalized and excluded in LGBTQ communities, individualizing problems to specific groups or individuals such as trans-people or those with mental health issues (see also Browne & Bakshi, 2013).

Broader heteronormative orders remain unquestioned in framing other places as 'the problem' or having 'problems'. Using a decolonial lens that contests forward/backward progress narratives are not to negate the impacts of juridico-political regimes, which, as we will show in Chapter 3 and have discussed elsewhere based on participants' experiences, have significant effects (see Browne, Banerjea et al., 2021). Instead, it is to note how the other plays a part in making sense of liveabilities in the creation of sexual and gendered lives, politics and activisms. A decolonial lens of liveabilities then asks for both nuance and recognition of the power relations that create differential precarity – in part through the creation of other people, in other places. Transnational work such as this book and its making can seek to question the positioning of nation-states, cultures and places within a hierarchical logic. It is about disrupting Global North/Global South divides and intervening into debates that hierarchize 'Western democracies' as spaces of inclusion, whilst simultaneously vilifying exotic 'others' as 'inherently homophobic' and synonymous with 'backwardness' (Kulpa & Mizielinskia, 2011; Puar, 2007). It is clear that these divides and presumptions are shaping contemporary LGBTQ politics 'here' and 'there', ignoring and individualizing ongoing marginalizations and discriminations here, whilst seeking to 'help' (save?) 'there'.

We do not deny the materialities of differential precarity, which we discuss throughout this book. It is, however, to highlight the mutual transnational constitution of sexual (and gendered) politics and lives, including through interpretations of colonial geopolitical framings of modern liberal subjects who can only exist in certain places. Participants speaking of elsewhere as worse than here recreate their lives as 'more liveable'. This perspective reiterates Global North/Global South rural/urban and interprets these differentiations as central to how 'here' is perceived and lived.

Conclusion

At the end of our argument to decolonize sexuality rights discourses, we ask in a self-introspection mode if our work reproduces what we seek to dismantle. We may not have a satisfactory answer to this question because both of us are imbricated in colonial and colonizing trajectories of intellectual production. By proposing liveability as a decolonial option, we know that we are still primarily depending on concepts and language produced in the Anglo-American English-speaking world. Yet, to deal with everyday microaggressions within university settings, the ever-increasing limited spaces for critical academic work to thrive against contestations of its validity and place in the university, and the closing in of the rights bearing free queer subject, it is imperative to create counter-narratives from all sides, with whatever concept and collaborations hold critical potential. For us, the usage of liveability emerged at a certain point through a conversation both of us were having, which neither binds nor limits us to deploy others to interrupt hegemonic discourses about the sexual subject. Liveability is therefore not the key, not a panacea but an option, an optic and a possibility.

Extending liveability through a decolonial lens works to contest hegemonic thinking that drives sexual and gender rights agendas, politics and research. Liveability as a decolonial option has the potential to address the limits of uninterrogated equality-based agendas which seek to recognize, codify and act for and upon marginalized subjects, even when some of these subjects are incorporated into the liberal assimilationist imaginary. The British and Indian Queer figures are often presented as opposites, in comparative frames, and in that comparison the colonial relationship is reformed. 'Here' and 'there' then are products of elaborate colonial schemas (modern/traditional, civilized/barbarian, progressive/backward) along which regions and populations are placed, always indicating a chronological motion of arrival to modernity civilization, progress. The solidarities that can be forged through sharing knowledge and experiences around liveabilities across academia and activism and through places of colonial difference give us hope and reasons for optimism.

Juridico-political forms of power, to which we now turn, are not the only epistemic sites that organize our experiences and can promise liberation from our colonial pasts and reworked colonial present. Activisms in India that seek to recognize kinship in more queer terms, beyond same-sex couples, emphasize the considerations, potentials and possibilities that may encompass lives that (are not yet) realized. We explore these liveabilities further in Chapter 4. With our focus on liveability through a different analysis of space and time, we are not saying that this is the only counter-hegemonic lens or that should be now universally deployed; there can be others as well. The point is, whatever lens we decide to use and from within our intellectual and material contexts, it is crucial to question how our actions and presumptions, including 'progressive sexual politics', can reproduce colonial relations of power or help to create forms of knowledge that are otherwise subsumed within such relations. Thus, how the un/acceptable and the un/intelligible are lived out, and how what is not lived out, what is not liveable, also leave its mark as a mode of un/intelligibility. If one lives according to rationality, what forms of 'life' come to haunt that mode of rationality as its outside, and how do those not liveable modes vacillate between what is 'here' and what is 'there' refusing geopolitical distinctions?

3

Structures of inclusion: Within and beyond sexualities and gender equalities and rights

Introduction

This chapter developing from discussions of liveabilities and decoloniality interrogates the inclusion/exclusion dualism in relation to the here/there narrative to address how structures of inclusion under equalities legislation are both necessary and problematic in the pursuit of liveable lives. Contemporary academic work in gender-sexuality studies has brought into question inclusions, particularly those obtained through equalities legislation. For example, critical framings of safety see legislative change as inadequate without social transformation (Browne et al., 2011; Hubbard, 2013; Perry, 2002), and supposedly inclusive legislation can reiterate existing power relations creating new (stigmatized) others, and demand sameness/normalizations that undermine the differences that constitute vibrant societies (Duggan, 2002; Richardson, 2005; Richardson & Monro, 2012). Those voices that have for years been left out of Brahmanical academic structures but are critical to activisms and theorizations of gender-sexuality, caste and class in the social have also argued consistently that legal changes are meaningless unless there are changes in mindsets (Ambedkar, 1936; Revathi, 2016). It is no surprise then that those considering equalities legislation and expected freedoms show that the presence and absence of equalities laws do not directly map people's everyday experiences, desires or hopes. This chapter lays out a framework of liveability that can hold and inhabit a complex engagement with the juridico-political. We offer a nuanced positioning that neither ties itself to legislative changes as a panacea or measure of what makes a life a life for LGBTQ people nor does it negate its importance. Instead, it recognizes the complexities of everyday lived experiences in and through legislation/perceptions of societal and familial acceptance and identifies their cracks and fissures.

Building on the decolonial readings of sexualities and genders in Chapter 2, we begin by contesting the hierarchization of the UK by scrutinizing the implementation of the landmark Equality Act 2010 and, to a lesser extent, the Marriage (Same-Sex Couples) Act 2013, both of which are supposed markers of the UK/Great Britain as 'leading the way' (see also Browne et al., 2016; Nash & Browne, 2020 for a detailed analysis). The section following this will engage with select Indian news reports to gauge the visible public discourse concerning S 377 and responses around that. We follow up data from our participants that discuss experiences, perceptions of living and activisms to further push the boundaries of 'a here that is fine' versus 'a there that is not'. The chapter will conclude with aspirations to live and survive with legislative changes in ways that note their importance, without negating their limitations.

Implementing legislation: Living up to progress narratives?

The Equalities Act 2010 was heralded in the UK to culminate New Labour's drive towards equalities (Browne & Bakshi, 2013). It was seen as consolidating the gains made legislatively by the left-centre leaning party, although it was given cross-party support. The Equality

Act 2010 named nine protected characteristics, including sexual orientation and gender reassignment.[1] This legislation was then translated into 'Specific Duties of the Public Sector' that required the public sector to enact the provisions of the Equality Act in specific ways (Equality Act 2010 Specific Duties Regulations 2011). Focusing on whether and how these duties were enacted offers direct insight into local governments tasked with implementing key areas of the legislation and measuring and publicizing their progress in doing so.[2]

In our review of English local authorities' implementation of their LGBTQ-related duties under the Equality Act 2010, more than half of local authorities (53 per cent, n. 188) were not adhering to or implementing the Specific Duties of the Equality Act 2010 and associated Government Equalities Office guidance (2011). These Equalities duties were broader than LGBTQ. However, such an absence indicated the limits of legislative implementation at the local government level. Only twenty councils (6 per cent of all councils) had Equality Objectives aimed explicitly at LGBTQ people during the first phase of our project work (2014/15). Only one council had set an Equality Objective specifically regarding trans-people (as opposed to more general LGBTQ equalities work). This indicates a lack of attention to LGBTQ people more broadly, and a focus on 'sexual orientation', rather than 'gender reassignment'- when setting goals for local government to fulfil their public sector duties towards LGBTQ people.[3] While we can be critical of aspects such as the effectiveness of local government actions, the requirement for objectives and other critiques of neoliberal governance, the absence of these is also significant. It indicates a lack of attention to LGBTQ lives, even where progressive social legislation and public sector duties are established nationally and celebrated internationally. It points directly to how these legislative changes fail to be implemented while simultaneously being used as national progress measures compared with other 'failing'/'backward' nation states. Undermining the presumed efficacy of these legislations through exploring the implementation at the local government level does not contest the cultural and individual shifts they can afford. However, it does require a reconsideration of comparative assessments and associated claims to 'civilization' and 'inclusion'.

In contrast to LGBTQ equalities work and linking directly to debates regarding the normalization of certain relationship forms and their validation through same-sex marriage (Duggan, 2002; Harding & Peel, 2006; Warner, 1999a, 1999b), far more local governments incorporated information about civil partnerships and marriage. Of the 153 councils (43 per cent of all local government authorities surveyed) who provided marriage services in 2014/15, 62 (41 per cent of eligible councils, including four that lacked any details on civil partnerships and/or same-sex marriage) had no details about converting existing civil partnerships to same-sex marriages, an option available in England and Wales from December 2014. During the second phase of our work (2016), many of these councils had updated their websites. Only twenty-four (16 per cent of eligible councils) were found not to provide details of civil partnerships, same-sex marriages and conversion of the former to the latter. Of those councils providing complete information regarding same-sex marriages, civil partnerships and the conversion of civil partnerships to same-sex marriages (129 out of the 153 eligible), twenty-one did not report any LGBTQ equality work, and nineteen were assessed as undertaking weak/limited LGBTQ equality work. Thus, 31 per cent (n. 40) of those councils fully promoting same-sex marriage are either doing no LGBTQ work or only limited LGBTQ work in the broader equalities arena of local government. This establishes an inconsistency in response to different pieces of legislation addressing LGBTQ issues. It reveals that while some legislation around what can be termed homonormative inclusions (Duggan, 2002) is widely celebrated and implemented, other LGBTQ work that is more complex and that involves issues of multiple and ongoing marginalizations may be sidelined through the poor implementation of supposedly mandatory legislative duties.

In 2015, there were significant cuts to UK public sector funding and, specifically, local government (Munro & Richardson, 2014). It was clear that for some, equalities broadly and LGBTQ-specific work were viewed as superfluous during these times, in favour of targeting resources in other areas (Munro & Richardson, 2014) and reiterating specific normativities and narratives in discussions of LGBTQ equalities (Lawrence & Taylor, 2020). This indicates a disconnect between the seeming value placed in international rankings for the UK and the on-the-ground engagements with LGBTQ equalities in ways that sought to address exclusions and marginalizations, particularly for the most vulnerable LGBTQ people who may well be reliant on state support and local government action. However, in our project's contact with some local authorities, they went beyond suggesting that this issue was tangential to other vital roles that local government needed to play. Instead, they challenged or resisted equalities work as unnecessary (see also Nash & Browne, 2020). Some local government replies to our requests for information were at pains to emphasize that they were *not legislatively* required to fulfil these duties, treating them as optional extras rather than integral to local government work in their communities.

While the UK was being lauded for its equalities legislation, and in 2015 topping the ILGA Europe rainbow list (ILGA Europe, 2015), exploring local government implementation paints a different picture. Whilst many local authorities embraced same-sex marriages, this was not reconciled with equalities work that required change, effort and attention during a period of funding cuts and staff shortages. Authorities could be focused on workloads, accusations of political correctness and indeed 'treating everyone the same' to refuse to engage with broader LGBTQ equalities initiatives. Thus, these data point to the requirement to engage with more than legislation on the statute book, but also the processes of implementing and living these laws. Such data question the categorization of England (and the broader UK) as uniformly 'advanced', 'progressive', 'equal' or a 'world we have won'.

Narratives of progress will usually raise issues of incorrect implementation that need to be fixed to retain their stand. We want to highlight the futility of comparison scales on which forward/backward categorizations rely. Such scales are always faulty, always needing to be fixed according to the larger juridico-political and everyday life contexts within which they operate. Using them to compare nations is futile precisely because they are constructed through imaginaries of comparison, in which fixing becomes a goal to perfect that scale, rather than to discard it and focus on lives that need to benefit from affirmative policymaking. To further this discussion, we turn to the landscape in India to examine the effects of S 377 on select media discourses.

Postcolonial legalities: Recognition and rights in 'backward' states

The reinstatement of S 377 on 11 December 2013, through the setting aside of the 2009 Naz Foundation, generated a lot of publicity. We undertook a temporal media analysis, focusing on English language news reports around S 377 in some national and regional daily newspapers from 2009 to 2013. The purpose of this was to gauge the visible public discourse concerning S 377 and responses around that. As this section will demonstrate, the question of recognition and rights cannot be read in a linear temporal fashion, i.e. from backward to forward. Legal reforms in India 'are a result of complex social and legal struggles that produce ambivalent and diverse effects' (Dhawan, 2016: 64). Thus, equating reform as forward and its absence as backward closes off nuanced understanding at best and is a colonial reading at worst.

Overall, there was a more LGBTQ-friendly tone after the 2009 Naz Judgement, which dissipated after the 2013 Delhi High Court judgement. Yet, even post 2009, celebratory reports in the news coverage existed alongside ongoing discriminatory and oppressive statements targeted at LGBTQ people, for example, by 'khaps'[4] in northwest India and the refusal of self-identified gay men at a blood bank in a public hospital in Delhi.[5]

The question of legal recognition and rights in news reports was often situated within a parallel discussion of the 'Indianness' of homosexuality. Some newspapers had focused on homosexuality in history as a kind of legitimizing move for persons who say it is a non-Indian issue. References to Khajuraho and Konarak temples[6] where homoerotic sculptures reside were linked to an understanding that homosexuality is part of the nation's heritage (Pattanaik, 2019). These reports were validated further by Ruth Vanita's (2011) discussion of queer love and marriage legalities in Indian histories.[7] Trying to prove that homosexuality is a 'natural phenomenon', these articles went to great lengths to justify how homosexuality is ancient and thus part of Hinduism. Reading homosexuality as part of Hinduism while legitimizing homoerotic behaviour is also problematic, as its caste-ist frame is left uninterrogated. So, while this linkage between ancient and medieval Hindu pasts has served to decolonize homoeroticism in a literal sense, i.e. that homosexuality is not a western import, it has simultaneously left its caste-ist base unexamined.

A second angle that emerged through this media analysis was health. Using the terms 'gay' and 'trans community', some reports (Mudur, 2013; Yengkhom, 2009) focused on how a lack of HIV/AIDS awareness has led to a growth in the number of reported cases, increased substance abuse and mental health issues, including depression due to violence and related fear.

We came across four reports highlighting gay and lesbian couples 'marrying' or wanting to 'marry'[8] after the Delhi High Court verdict. Marriage has always been a contentious space for concern and discussion within the larger LGBTQ community, given its liberatory potential[9] and normative underpinnings; the 2009 judgement seemed to have launched some of these discussions into middle-class homes. However, post 11 December 2013, the tone of these reports changed, as marriage became sidelined to be replaced again by the question of (re)criminalization.

Social stigma and violence in the workplace and mention of death by suicides of lesbian and trans-people were interrelated realities that recurred in twenty-seven of the reports. Examples of direct and indirect aggression were tied to gradations of violence along class and caste lines and the marginalization of trans-people within the larger LGBTQ movement. Several of the reports, while referring to the 2009 verdict, did discuss how laws can only go so far in effecting social change. To this was added the question of religion. While on the one hand, some reports were referring to the place of same-sex love within Hindu texts, on the other, these same reports were voicing the concerns of Hindu priests and political leaders who labelled homosexuality as a Western concept and practice. Beyond Hindu considerations, there was little reporting on the voices of Muslim religious leaders; instead, reports purported that Islam does not condone homosexuality. However, the voices of Christian priests and their dilemma with the LGBTQ movement were highlighted. For instance, it was reported that churches in the state of Mizoram have tried to discourage homosexuality amongst their members and tried to come together to protest against the verdict (Times of India, 2010). Catholic churches were also reported to stand against adoption rights for same-sex couples or even single men and women. Further, an astrologer Suresh Koushal who was one of the main petitioners against the Delhi High Court verdict, in an interview with *The Hindu* talked about his decision to challenge the verdict, going into detail about how 'using the backside' (anal sex) is like 'reversing the motion of earth' when he was asked about the rights of trans-people (Pisharoty, 2013). In the same interview, Koushal tried to explain how taking away S 377 would wreak havoc as there would be nobody to 'control them':

> I begged the court to look at some important issues, like, to think about what would happen in the hostels, how rich families will exploit their servants, *koi rokne wala nahi hoga* (there won't be anybody to stop them.), *un ko kaun control karega?* (Who will control them?). It is also directly linked to our national security. Lakhs of jawans[10] and defence personnel stay away from their families to safeguard our borders and important places. If Section 377 is lifted, they would miss their partners and get into consensual relationships with each other. What happens in the long run … we might lose a battle.

The 2013 verdict and its placement within the 2014 election that brought the Bharatiya Janata Party (BJP)[11] into power found a place in some articles talking about quashed hopes of a parliamentary amendment to read down S 377. A large number of articles focused exclusively on how the government was trying to handle situations related to LGBTQ lives. There were quite a few articles and reports that show the various national political parties and ruling government's reaction[12] over the years from 2009 to 2014 that are supportive of LGBTQ rights, whilst at other times contesting these. In 2009 when the Delhi High Court verdict overturning S 377 was passed, the Congress government was undecided about supporting the petitioner. Later because of the impending loss in the Lok Sabha election, Congress wanted to gain confidence with LGBTQ voters. By the time the appeal was heard in Supreme Court in 2013, a disparate view across the government had illustrated the incoherence we also saw in the UK implementation. While the law minister was for the Delhi High Court verdict, the health ministry opposed it with the Union Health Minister saying that men having sex with men is a disease and is unnatural (NDTV, 2011).

The 11 December 2013 judgement reinstating S 377 was followed by news articles on the inconsistency of law in India. Some government officials declined to comment, and others were vocal about their dissent against the 2013 reinstatement of S 377. The Attorney General of India at the time, G. E. Vahanvati, who represented the government's stand on the 2013 verdict, was a part of the entire trial. They opposed the Supreme Court's decision, saying that law cannot remain static, and Article 21 of the Constitution that protects life and personal liberty of the individual had received a new life with the 2009 Naz Judgement (Vahanvati, 2013). The Supreme Court's 2013 verdict was often critiqued by calling it a 'step backward'. Spanning across the day after the judgement, 12 December 2013 was a day for media discussion of the verdict where lawyers, activists, columnists and those from other walks of life sought to understand and make sense of the sudden shift in the judiciary position.

Overall, these media reports show how the larger juridico-political decisions around S 377 play out in complex and multifaceted ways. They refuse easy categorization as 'backward' by highlighting diverse reactions; yet, they also show the importance of legal reforms that cannot be set aside. The media and the influence of the juridico-political sphere do not determine the making of liveable lives, but they do play a role. Liveability thus cannot be reduced to legislation, but neither is it outside the realm of legal reforms. As we now turn to explore, this was apparent in how participants spoke of their desire for legislative change, opening questions regarding the experiences of such legislative changes within and beyond their local realization through governmental structures.

Hearts and minds are more than rights: Recognition and equality in India and the UK

Exploring the lived experiences of LGBTQ people in both England and India offers insights into how juridico-political structures recreate lives and their limitations in assuming that they determine lives. Working transnationally in this way emphasizes commonalities across places that indicate oppressions and marginalizations do not disappear with legislation, nor (as we will show in the next section) are they necessarily expected to even where this legislation is desired.

Focusing on juridico-political landscapes can overlook broader cultural changes that exceed legislation and that LGBTQ people in England identified as continuing to be important in an era of supposed LGBTQ equalities post same-sex marriage. Participants recognized that rational and emotional arguments that contested LGBTQ rights continued to form their experiences beyond legislative changes:

> The law may have changed but we continue to play catch up with hearts & minds
>
> (Project Workshop, England)

The change in English legislation was not seen as enough to change societal attitudes towards LGBTQ people. The idea of 'hearts and minds' points to the limitations of legal changes that do not change common-sense options and feelings. The hope and expectation of change from legislative inclusions were also understood as not necessarily pre-given. Instead, the disgust of LGBTQ lives, identities and practices was a fear that 'remained' for British participants:

> Susan: Legal things [are] changing, people can think that everything is okay just because people are married obviously, but you're living next door to a bigot or somebody that thinks it's disgusting. The issues still remain for people.
>
> (Project Workshop, England)

Our English participants noted that for some, same-sex marriage was seen as an endpoint in the legal recognition, especially for gay men and lesbians. Yet as Susan contended, this does not stop perceptions and attitudes of others affecting your life. Participants in Bengal also identified the limits of legislation as a means of protecting oneself from marginalization through exposure and societal reactions:

> Anita: Say a couple gets exposed, what would the law do? I am discounting the societal reaction, what can the law do?
>
> (In-depth interview, India)

Anita speaking both to the law and reactions towards LGBTQ people queries assumptions regarding the place of the law in changing everyday lives. She notes the limitations of enforcing the law in changing attitudes or perhaps 'hearts and minds', even where this legislation is not in place, she questions its possible effectiveness and impact on LGBTQ lives. Thus, legislation is not understood as offering a 'somewhere' to be satisfied. Where it exists or not, it does not promise the social acceptances, which are so desired by some LGBTQ people:

> NB: What is a good life?
> Ripu: Somewhere I would be satisfied with the life I am leading, satisfied with my work, attire … I want to live my life on my own terms and that would be a good life to live.
> SB: Like?
> Ripu: I want to have fun … I want to laugh, I want to cry when I want to … do what I feel like doing … but this life … I have never said this to anyone before … it's so painful to live at times … I cannot just up and leave if I want to, once I felt even death would be better …
> NB: This life?
> Ripu: A relationship with a woman, but it's not accepted … I cannot ask anyone why … I know why, but I cannot ask the question loudly … it's not a life I wanted … it's painful …
>
> (In-depth interview, India)

The pain of lacking acceptance and the inability to 'live my life on my own terms' can lead to the feeling that 'even death would be better' (Johnson, 2015; Johnson et al., 2007; Rivers et al., 2018). To ask 'loudly' why is not necessary, it is known and understood, reflecting the common-sense norms that create heteronormative spaces and lives (Browne, 2006).

The perceptions of bigotry and a lack of acceptance shaped people's lives and were informed by their experiences of everyday spaces. Safety, abuse and violence, and the fears of these are key issues for LGBTQ people (Browne & Bakshi, 2013; Perry, 2002) emerging across a variety of spaces:

> Shelley: So she [ex-partner] was quite fearful when the kids were around about how we ought to hide our sexuality … I wanted to keep the children feeling safe. I was alright with that. I had other kinds of anxieties about not feeling physically very safe in the town because of people's attitudes in the town and because it was quite rough and I didn't want to get my head kicked in.
>
> (Project Workshop, England)

Shelley highlights the fear around publicly expressing sexualities that can go beyond the self and incorporate fears for others, including children, whose safety can be compromised. The attitudes of people where she lived played a significant role in policing her behaviour and the fears that she felt. This was mirrored in the conversations in India, too, where relationships are not recognized because of safety fears and the effect this has in creating precarious and vulnerable lives. In the words of Ishika and Vaibhavi:

> Ishika: Correct. That lack of safe space, if you cannot recognise your relationship or your partner cannot recognise you, it makes us even more of a loner. It makes us … Vulnerable, constricted …
>
> (In-depth interview, India)

> Vaibhavi: As same-sex lovers, we are discriminated a lot out in public and that exacerbates the insecurity we already feel … so it does matter … we are easily identified especially where our orientation matters. This is our societal norms, you know, where we have been taught that only a man and a woman can stay in a park or only they can go for grocery, two women or two men cannot go holding hands … whenever R and I go out, we are looked at with such derision, it is disconcerting … we both feel that … we cannot even hold our hands, who wants to point oneself out in the open! We don't want confrontations […] so these things hurt. Say we have gone to a restaurant, the waiter is observing both of us like we belong to a zoo or something or so there are so many places of discriminations now if either R or I had a man with us, the same people would have welcomed us with open arms.
>
> (In-depth interview, India)

These experiences in both Bengal and England point to othering and a lack of safety in public places where sexual expressions are heavily policed and women fear violence, for both themselves and others. These collective feelings do not solely revolve around the safety of a couple in public spaces, but also emphasize the need for members of a collective to worry about each other:

> Akanksha: I am not worried about myself, because I don't know what danger I might be in, and if my orientation creates some problem, I don't think it would affect me much, but other people with the same orientation are afraid of being persecuted so that still affects me.
>
> NB: when you said violence is on the rise in West Bengal, especially on women, so since you identify yourself as a woman …
>
> Akanksha: Yes, absolutely. I definitely identify myself as a woman, but I think I am more vulnerable since I am not only a woman, but a homosexual woman. I am almost fifty now, I probably

won't have to face physical violence at my age. Not because I am physically strong, but perhaps my socio-economic status acts as a safeguard.

(In-depth interview, India)

Legislative change can acknowledge that women and other LGBTQ people are vulnerable, but societal attitudes are key to the lived experiences of LGBTQ people. 'Hearts and minds' may not be changed through legal changes, and the ongoing experiences and the creations of vulnerabilities and precarities through fear and violence can remain core to LGBTQ lives. Importantly, the scale and intensity of such violence, including its fear, can be mediated by one's caste, class and racial background. It is not uniform.

Narratives and fear of physical violence were more apparent in the conversations in India. Yet in all the interactions and conversations, experiences of physical violence were supplemented with the subtle interactions and relations between people in everyday lives that create conditions for violence and discrimination. English participants spoke of continuing to feel othered, different and fearful. For Franco, a liveable life would refuse labels and their divisiveness as he understood it; instead, there would be further possibilities of creating connections with other people:

Franco: I think that a life which is a hundred per cent liveable, you just don't think about the fact that you're gay, you know, you stop labelling yourself like in general.

… Every time we meet someone, I think all of us spend at least a few seconds trying to decide whether that person is going to be homophobic or not so that you know exactly what can come out of your mouth and what cannot and like how much you can move your arms or how much you cannot. …

Walking into a straight club is like walking into the closet. I just really feel that horrible feeling of shame and I think people don't care about that and that's not something that's spoken about because, 'Oh yeah. It's fine now because I don't care if you're getting married.' I'm like, 'Well it's not completely fine because we wouldn't feel that if it was'. And people are like, 'Well why do you have your own clubs? We should all just mix.' And I'm like, 'Because I still need that feeling of safety and that tells me that okay, so the bigger stuff like being beaten up in the street and the more obvious displays of hate aren't there, but there are these really underlying things'.

(Project Workshop, England)

Having to consider and be aware 'that you are gay' is a moment of unwelcome difference for Franco. For Franco, there are underlying things that he still contends with during his social life, going out to straight bars, and the continued feelings of safety in clubs that feel like 'our own' (Gorman-Murray & Nash, 2014, 2017; Nash, 2013; Nash & Gorman-Murray, 2014, 2015). His narrative speaks of fear, vigilance and awareness of the ongoing fear of homonegativity and homophobia that defines daily interactions (Browne, 2007a), the 'underlying things' that remain a feature of LGBTQ people's lives even when legislations are in place, including around hate crimes:

> Lorretta: So I feel like they all feed each other and I do feel like, yeah, maybe there's less to fight in terms of you have less chances to get murdered in the street because you're gay, but in the meantime there are less things I feel they're just more subtle and people tend to give up about it because they feel like it's becoming okay but I feel like this one is actually going to come back.
>
> Leo: I think you're absolutely right. I think that's when people say to us about, you know, we've got an LGBT forum, we've got Pride, you know, 'Why do you do that anymore? Don't need that anymore. You don't march, okay, have a party instead' ... We have some people sort of think, 'Well you don't need that kind of support anymore. You've got what you need. You're where you want to be', but we do need to keep an eye on things ... I think we need to just watch that plate spinning on

the stick and just keep that going because as soon as we take our eyes of that, it's going to crash, and that's what worries me.
(Project Workshop, England)

Noting the feeling that things are 'becoming ok', Lorretta's concern is also that 'this one is actually going to come back'. She and other participants saw the ongoing stigmatization of LGBTQ people as a necessary addendum to the idea that there has been successful and irrevocable social, legal and political change to the benefit of all LGBTQ people in Great Britain. This leads to less 'chances' of 'murder' but the subtle othering and contestations of the liveabilities of LGBTQ people remain in question. If taken seriously such moments of othering could rework the terms of the debates and associated activisms that refuse to see the battle as 'won' and insist instead on the place and importance LGBTQ spaces and events, such as Pride. More than this, attention to the subtle, indicates that attention and vigilance remain necessary, as there is no guarantee as to the longevity of legislative changes (see Nash & Browne, 2020).

The subtle has ongoing effects on people's lives in terms of where they will and will not go and how they feel after these encounters (see also Browne et al., 2011; Browne & Bakshi, 2013). Limiting understandings of LGBTQ equalities to not being murdered or having same-sex marriage affects how you can live your life, with negative experiences being fearfully expected. What our work points to is how transnationally, LGBTQ people regardless of legislative context continued to be subject of humiliating and difficult experiences, often seemingly brushed off as a 'joke'. We draw attention to some extended excerpts of conversations around this:

> Denise: Even certain like groups of people that I'll completely avoid. Even just a normal pub. I'll get stressed out in certain situations like work makes me nervous sometimes. That sort of thing ... Whatever it is, if it impacts upon your liveability or

quality of life, then it's a problem. Like that's how you should define it and for me personally anything, like any banter about my sexuality from someone … that is just not okay and that does impact your liveability because you don't just experience that at the office and then go home and carry on with your life. That stays with you for a long time because for your next job or your training day or a new colleague arrives, you think, 'Oh god. I've got to do it all over again.'

Sam: There are things that seep through but then it's almost like they're accepted in some way. Like because we're all grown adults, you know, we assume that we can all take a joke and stuff like that but it's not talked about enough … What is actually quite offensive and what maybe people should take back in context?

Denise: There's homophobia in totally different ways. You're completely right. Like at work. I always feel the need now to go into work and you're like, 'Hi. How are you?'. I'm like, 'Hi. I'm a lesbian.' [Laughs] Let's just do that really quickly because then I can- It's just out there then and then the banter can commence where I will happily join in taking the piss out of myself because it's easier than being like, 'Please don't offend me because that's really hurtful'. Like I had a manager, a professional manager, refer to me always never by my name, but always as lezzer, and I laughed at that. Like, 'Yeah. Lezzer! Fine. Cool', but then I look back at that and I'm like, 'That's not fine. That's really not fine', that type of homophobia absolutely exists. As one person you're vulnerable. You go along with it because you're like, 'I don't know how to challenge this in a way we don't come across as an angry lesbian'. You just don't want to be a stereotype because people automatically think if you start ranting, 'Oh angry lesbian. Man-hater.'

Franco: I think that those are the type of things that once you come out and you go through the ups and downs, eventually you are comfortable with yourself, and you can take a joke and almost like you generally don't care, because it can actually be

a genuine joke that doesn't come from a place of, you know, of-
[...] They are probably not even actually trying to discriminate.
People don't realise that because sometimes people think, you
know, like it's fine, you know, it's just a joke, but it can be a joke
to me but like there's other people that would be really upset
by that.
Nadine: But why is homosexuality a joke? Like why is that a joke?
I don't understand that. We don't be like, 'Oh those straight
people'. But like it's not a thing, is it?

(Project Workshop, England)

Ishika: No, not then, but now I understand. It's against my
principles ... I will not go out on a drink with whoever because
that person is my client. They can be whoever; if I don't want
to go, it's my choice. And obviously at my workspace, my
sexuality ... because I have never been very shh shh about
it ... they are very ... it has turned into kind of a private
joke sometimes. Like, sometimes everybody is okay ... you
are like this, very good, we are very supportive, we are like
this supportive people, but suddenly ... some below the belt
jokes and you know they are about you. At that point you feel
very hurt, that these are the people ... I have not led a very
hypocritical life; I could have hidden my whatever ... I have
chosen not to .... So if you have to say something, if you have
any opinion, say that on my face instead of cracking some
private joke and trying to ... me, don't do that. It's hurtful,
it's very insensitive, it's uneducated and I absolutely get very
furious about it.

(Project Workshop, India[13])

These quotes from both England and Bengal point to how the idea of a sexual or gender identity as part of a joke has effects in liveabilities. Sexual and gender differences continue to be seen, even in places where we supposedly have 'won'. In spaces where people are ostensibly 'supportive', there continues to be an issue with who is ridiculed and how. These quotes invoke the everyday realities of lives that may not be noticed and can indeed be presumed to be 'acceptance'. But being the object and subject of a joke whether you are involved or not can have damaging effects that continue to render you other, different and less than those for who 'it is not a thing'. These experiences, as part of the everyday, 'stay with you' well beyond the spaces in which such 'banter' was encountered. The idea of a sexual or gender identity as part of a joke indicates how these differences continue to be seen.

This is the case in homo- and trans-positive juridico-political spaces where people are ostensibly 'supportive'; there continues to be an issue with who is ridiculed and how.

Mutual understanding and love, beyond same-sex marriage as the pinnacle of LG(BTQ) equalities?

Same-sex marriage is often positioned in national comparisons and popular culture as a key indicator of 'progress' and 'civilization'. Situated on a linear temporal scale, it can be seen as a marker of 'full equality' for LGBTQ people. Yet, in our research, LGBTQ people also pointed to the moments when inclusions such as same-sex marriage can make life *less* liveable for LGBTQ people:

> Margaret: With gay marriage, I mean it might make it easier to be part of society if you're gay and you're married but I mean what about gay people that don't want to get married or never wanted to get married ... what if I actually deviate from certain norms and actually deviate myself from a lot of norms which makes my life not liveable? ... What's the standard that I have to fit? If I fit the homonormative standard like of England for instance and I get married and I have kids no matter if I marry someone of the same gender I'll be fine, but what if I don't want to do that? Then my life is not liveable

> anymore. ... All these kind of alternative options that have once been available, it maybe will start to disappear because marriage will become the goal. ... We've got equality, like and then yeah internally maybe it gets less liveable. Maybe it gets harder even if externally it's getting easier. Not that the two are mutually exclusive in any way.
>
> (Project Workshop, England)

Margaret and others in the English workshops saw the same-sex marriage legislation as core to supposed societal acceptance, for some. Yet, Margaret notes the paradox of lives getting easier, and more difficult in ways that are not mutually exclusive but ask for more than legislative change. In this case, happiness regarding the existence of same-sex marriage in 'some places' was tempered against the ways in which it reconstructed normative coupled family relations as the pinnacle (see Wilkinson, 2012).

This is not about rejecting same-sex marriage, per se, but recognizing that positive legislation supposedly for all LGBTQ people may result in normative violence for some (see Sears, 2005; Warner, 1999a, 1999b; Richardson, 2017). A new order can be created such that some who were once sexual and gender dissidents are now part of this 'new normal', leaving others who remain anti-normative and are potentially more vulnerable because LGBTQ people are now seemingly 'equal' in the eyes of the law (Duggan, 2002; Sears, 2005). This can be a difficult conundrum when you benefit from these structures and must buy into them to make your life liveable, but fundamentally you disagree with these 'ethics of inclusion':

> As someone who doesn't believe in marriage, I was forced to enter into the institution in order to remain with my partner in the UK. I'm lucky enough to have the opportunity to do so given the laws have changed to allow it but I struggle with the ethics of inclusion – the state deciding whose relationships are and are not legitimate.
>
> (Questionnaire data)

This questionnaire response points to the aspiration for more than those LGBTQ people who are 'lucky'. It asks for a collective response that sees institutions such as marriage that legitimize some relationships offering benefits and possibilities, whilst negating others (for example single people, see Wilkinson, 2012). Same-sex marriage and other normative inclusions may well not be desired. Indeed, in contrast with other rights and protections, it can be seen as superfluous, for some:

> SB: If same-sex marriage were to be legalised in our country, would you get married?
> Pakhi: No, I don't want to ... two people can live together with mutual understanding and love without getting married.
> (In-depth interview, India)

Pakhi does not require marriage, and is not interested in state recognition and engagement. Instead, she aspires to a collective aspiration that does not leave certain queers 'out in the cold' (Sears, 2005). She asks for more than state-sanctioned coupling, a relationship that allows for 'mutual understanding and love' to live together 'without getting married'. We might extend this to ask for this also beyond coupledom; to include friendships and queer-ed kin and relationalities see for example queer kinship discussions (Dahl & Gabb, 2019; Mizielińska et al., 2018; Wilkinson, 2012).

Such a conceptualization of mutual understanding and love was also apparent where LGBTQ people were critical of the diversity and complexities of LGBTQ communities that were approached in tickbox fashion by legislators and policymakers:

> Gordon: We put ourselves under this one homogenous group as if we all fit into that neat little box. And unfortunately, that manifests itself in services who say, 'Right. We've done the LGBT bit so we can tick a box on equality impact assessment[14]', and you're going, 'Have you? How did you do that then?' 'Well we've me the needs of

LGBT people.' 'Tell me how you've done that? So how have you met the needs of trans men as opposed to trans women? How have you met the needs of lesbians that are very different to gay men and gay men who are different to bisexuals? How have you done that?' And you can see them thinking, 'Oh shit. I'm in trouble here', because they're not the same.

(Project Workshop, England)

Engaging with the diversity of LGBTQ people's lives, and the complexities of legislative inclusions that normalize, offers possibilities and limitations. LGBTQ is not a homogeneous grouping, and accounting for different identities and lives asks for more than tickboxes. It asks for a recognition of difference, of understanding and of meaningful change.

Conversely, the possibilities afforded by legislative change even where it homogenizes, are also apparent where people can be 'well' without them, even as they are desired:

How are you doing as a lesbian/bisexual/transgender person? (tick on *lesbian*)

We live in a society, therefore our happiness and sadness depends on society's vision of life, if you look at it from this angle then sometimes I feel lonely and friendless.

But personally I do have a partner and she is perfect. If you look at it from this perspective then I am doing well. 'I am doing well these days.'

(Project Workshop, India)

'Society's vision of life' can be seen as the happy life promised through adherence to heterosexual orders, and temporalities (Ahmed, 2007). Such normativities create 'loneliness and friendless' lives for those who do not conform, who queer these expectations, and yet these lives can be full and liveable through partners who are considered 'perfect'. Larger social normativities and disapproval then are also limited in understanding what makes life liveable. Indeed, taking steps that are problematic for social normativities, which can further experiences of marginalization, exclusion and rejections, can also create wellness as minds and bodies align:

> How are you doing as a lesbian/bisexual/transgender person?
> If you mean a man residing within a female body is a transgender then before 9.11.15 I was that and I was very unwell mentally. After the surgery my mind and body are balanced and I am doing much better. That I can now identify as a male makes me very happy. I don't feel shy to stand in front of a mirror, I don't feel shy standing in front of other women and look for a life partner in them.
> (Project Workshop, India)

Focusing on liveabilities enables access to the limits of legislative equalities as well as experiences, often residing in the subtle that exceed juridico-political intelligibilities. Conversely, it also facilitates engagements with where lives can be well, even where social relations feel oppressive and marginalizing. Juxtaposing these poses specific questions to how legislative equalities and same-sex marriage can be both oppressive seeking instead understanding and love with the other. Yet, as we now turn to show, this conclusion does not acknowledge the *potentials* of legislative changes and their role in social attitudes and everyday lives.

The complex significance of legislation

We finish this chapter where once we might have started it, with the import of legislative rights, especially in a context of right-wing fundamentalism in India. We do so because too often the critiques of these rights, including our own, can overshadow their import by noting it and then pointing to the limits and issues. Yet from our interactions with our participants, particularly with those in India, it was clear that legislations are important and that their existence, in a form that does justice to a life worth living, does make a difference. Thus, whilst liveability cannot be reduced to legislation and we need to be wary of the ways in which legislative equalities are used to reiterate relational hierarchies in individual, collective and post-colonial, geopolitical contexts, comprehensive inclusive legislations matter especially to counter homogenizing juridico-political regimes. Their import in the creation of liveabilities cannot be overlooked or negated through these critiques.

In many of the interactions with participants in India their well-being and therefore liveability were linked to rights and the right-wing social political climate in which they existed:

> Q: How are you doing as a lesbian/bisexual/transgender person?
> The political and social climate we inhabit right now, and the pressure my friends and I face because of our gender-sexuality identity affects me. This socio-political surroundings don't keep me well. Because the state still hold 377, this keeps me unwell.
> (Project Workshop, India)

The 'holding' of 377 by a right state was a source of concern, as the fear of persecution, rather than prosecution, creates a 'pressure', as quite a few participants participate with other groups in creating critiques of homogenizing state narratives. For many others, a fear of being persecuted by family and colleagues with S 377 exists:

> Q: If you are unwell then what keeps you so?
> I am not doing well because my state doesn't recognise my rights. Inability to express my true identity in front of friends, colleagues, relatives keeps me unwell.
> (Project Workshop, India)

For some, the absence of positive legislation does not directly affect them, as it is often undercut by other privileges of class and caste, and yet there is an aspiration to be included in its ambit for a certain kind of assurance and protection, as it 'naturally' affects their lives.

> Q: Having laws or not having laws, that the state has criminalised you and has not given you any positive privileges either, does this bother you?
>
> Anamika: Yes of course it bothers me. At a personal level this has not affected me directly but it has influenced by thoughts. The way I think is affected by the laws … if I want to walk hand in hand with a girl there may be a problem, … Because at this moment I'm not staying with anyone it's not yet an issue in my life – but if I do then naturally my life will be affected. Directly it doesn't bother me but law is an issue in my life of course.
>
> (In-depth interview, India)

A deep-seated and heartfelt desire for state legislation was often seen as an important part of societal acceptances.

Linking rights to not being 'looked at in a bad way' was a critical leap in the hopes invested in legislative change. As one participant said:

> To stay well firstly I need rights. The same way a man-woman relationship is not looked at in a bad way a woman-woman relationship also shouldn't be.
>
> (Project Workshop, India)

These state rights were linked to acceptances, including being accepted from 'larger society' alongside family acceptances. Such acceptances were especially crucial in the case of lesbian identifying women who had the pressures of marriage, which will be elaborated on in the following chapter. Legal protection was thus seen as having effects that 'will keep me happy' (Participant 2, Project Workshop, India). Assertions of being 'allowed' 'to live with my identity' and to 'to live my life with my life-partner who is a girl with the L.B.[15] identity' were necessary to 'stay well' (Participant 4, Project Workshop, India). Hence, the co-existence of legal changes and family acceptances entangled in ways that could not be dismissed.

Legislative changes and reforms, while a part of activisms, did not however exist as an uncritical effort, to be consumed within those same familial systems that excluded them in the first place. Activism that sought more inclusive legislations was reliant on support systems that are painstakingly built outside of normative familial structures and legislative equalities. Speaking out against a discriminatory legislation requires a support system, as that critique is also tied to a larger critique of the state; at the same time, a support that one has painfully built with others has a separate meaning and entity that need not be guaranteed and/or maintained by the juridico-political order. The aspirational collective futures that included state-based legislative change for most were built through these support systems. As Malabika suggested, working on and for the collective against oppressive structures oppression can 'keep me alive through the pain':

> Let's say I have to fight on and on. There were four more people with me when this [Sappho] started, then they left for various reasons, and I knew I had to persevere for Sappho's future. There have been many ups and downs since then, now perhaps this is the very essence of community organisation that if it has been any other organisation, I could not have talked about it. This is not any other minority community ... it's the only one of its kind in Eastern India and I had to go on, you see? One day, we would not be there anymore, but the effort must go on. These challenges keep me alive through the pain.
>
> (In-depth interview, India)

Conclusion

There can be little doubt that certain forms of juridico-political inclusions across England and Wales and India structured through equalities legislations offer both limitations and possibilities. Legal reforms alone are never enough to overcome the means through which living, affective relationships and self-identifications are legitimated and/or stigmatized. The normalizations inherent in legislations such as same-sex marriage as has long been argued need to be sceptically and geographically assessed (Brown, 2009, 2012; Warner, 1999a, 1999b). And yet, activist efforts in India concerning legal reform were important to engage with as a means to open up spaces to counter discriminatory actions, violence and erasure. To expand the realm of legal reform may not equate simplistically with juridical cures, neither are they only normalizing. Those who ask for legal reform are often subjects that are formed through shaming, guilt, fear, pathologized by families, friends and at the receiving end of legislations that seek to favour some. Our conversations with the participants point to the complexity of legislative inclusions, which are deeply desired and fought for in India, but do not lead to utopia of necessarily liveable lives in England.

An engagement with equalities legislations and legal reforms thus means various kinds of interventions, often conflicting, which does not mean submission to the letter of the law. Drawing from Rodriguez (2014), we emphasize that instead of juridical cures, remaining open invites all of us implicated in these processes – caretakers, courts, scholars and activists – to rethink what support system means and can do to create liveable spaces. In this tension with the juridico-political order, formal recognition, while a site of power, is also generative in establishing valid lives in the everyday as well as media discourses. We conclude this chapter with the argument that legislation is a partial and generally unhelpful measure of liveabilities for LGBTQ people. Throughout the liveable lives research project, we have found that LGBTQ friendliness measures are problematic and exist mainly through discussions of homophobia (Browne et al., 2015; Rao, 2014). Even where equalities legislation exist, these are not consistently implemented. When the presumption is that legislative equality makes things 'okay' for LGBTQ people, there is a need to find new ways of talking about ongoing experiences of being othered. This goes beyond recognizing the moments and places of oppression, discrimination and exclusion that leave people 'furious' and, as we now turn to, considering what makes life liveable in ways that legislative changes can only partially address.

4
What makes a life liveable? (Non)normative lives, ordinary lives

Introduction

If, as we suggest in Chapter 3, legislation, whilst significant, is not a panacea for creating liveable lives, then exploring liveabilities beyond national-level legislations and instead in the realms of everyday lives offers an engagement with (non)normative LGBTQ identified lives on their terms. Refusing heteronormative time-spaces as conditions for a good life (Ahmed, 2010; Halberstam, 2005), this chapter will engage with the (non)normative to demonstrate the conditions and possibilities of ordinariness beyond the normative. Browne and Bakshi (2013) distinguish between ordinary, normal and normalization. As the previous chapter has shown, normalization is understood as adhering to a norm to become acceptable; when incorporated into legislative measures, it means exclusions for many and thus marginalization. In contrast, while potentially becoming normalized, a claim to ordinariness may also mean non-compliance to the standard and contingent upon specific geopolitical and historical contexts. Understood in this sense, an ordinary way of life will be unspecified, not necessarily predetermined. In other words, if there are many ways of becoming and being ordinary, ordinariness 'enables moves beyond the binaries of marginalisation/inclusion, normalisation/queer' (Browne & Bakshi, 2013: 191). The ordinary aspects of a liveable life pose profound questions about how we create sexual and gendered politics that refuse the normative and embrace the power of being ordinary.

In exploring how participants narrated their considerations of liveabilities with their everyday spaces, we examine and contest in turn the binaries of (a) living/surviving বেঁচে থাকা এবং টিকে থাকা (*benche thaka ebong tike thaka*/to live and to survive), (b) the normative and non-normative নিয়মতান্ত্রিক এবং নিয়মবিরোধী (*Niyomtantrik ebong niyombirodhee*) and (c) the ordinary and everyday সাধারণ আর গতানুগতিক (*sadharon ar gotanugotik*). Doing so reconstitutes understandings of the practices, material realities and aspirations of LGBTQ identifying people in our work, furthering our considerations of liveabilities through the possibilities it affords within and beyond critiquing oppressions.

'Flowing Upstream': Living and surviving/ বেঁচে থাকা এবং টিকে থাকা (*benche thaka ebong tike thaka*/to live and to survive)

Struggles, challenges and fights were key in how our interlocutors understood and expressed a complicated and multidirectional interplay between surviving and living. In *Undoing Gender*, Butler contends that the connection between liveability and survival is articulated through a process in which one tries to figure out ways to survive and persist. In other words, the journeys of persistence are also journeys of possibilities. Possibility is understood as 'an aspiration, something we might hope will be equitably distributed, something that might be socially secured, something that cannot be taken for granted ...' (Butler, 2004a: 31 cited in Rushing, 2010: 291). An otherwise mis- or non-recognized body attempts to achieve liveability through persistence and thereby becomes possible (2004a: 31). Butler points to this as a particular reality for those outside the heteronormative matrix, regularly violated and not considered within the ambit of liveability. This reality also marks the abject and those dispossessed (2004b, 2015). Survival and efforts to persist are connected to violation. To become possible then, persistence and avoidance of violence are key. This may involve conformity/complicity and pushing the terms through which one is made intelligible (Bell, 2008). As is well established in Butler's scholarship (1990, 1991, 2003), this reality is also a process of subjectification. Thus, to survive and live is also to become a gendered and sexualized subject.

In her *Notes toward a Performative Theory of Assembly* (2015), Butler uses a specific framing of the relation between survival and living:

> As I hope to have suggested, we cannot struggle for a good life, a liveable life, without meeting the requirements that allow for a body to persist. It is necessary to demand that bodies have what they need to survive, for survival is a precondition for all other claims we make. And yet, that demand proves insufficient since we survive precisely in order to live, and life, as much as it requires survival, must be *more* than survival in order to be livable. One can survive without being able to live one's life. And in some cases, it surely does not seem worth it to survive under such conditions. So, an overarching demand must be precisely for a livable life, that is, a life that can be lived.
>
> (208–9)

Here Butler suggests that life is 'more than' 'survival'. The relation she envisages arguably is that survival is a precursor to life, and it is the latter that should be strived for, not just survival. Some participants in England reiterated this:

> Clarence: I think a lot of it's just the basics that it takes for anyone. So like having some financial stability, having a roof over your head, being able to eat, being able to wash. Just the general stuff. Like there's a lot of homeless LGBT people. So a lot of that doesn't meet their basic needs so how can they have an enjoyable liveable life if you can't meet basic needs?
> Molly: I think mental health as well.

Clarence: Yeah. Mental health's quite a big one.
Molly: It's a big one.

(Project Workshop, England)

Separating 'basic needs' from an 'enjoyable liveable life' seeks to make a political statement about what people 'need' rather than what they might want. The 'they' interpellated here are not distant in the geographical senses as delineated in Chapter 2, but instead differentiated from Clarence and Molly through needs that are not met for them. This drives political discourses for 'them' who require support, but it also distances this support from enjoyment. Such distancing asks for political imperatives to increase survivability before liveability. It also can assume that survival is more pressing and until these issues are dealt with, the pursuit of an enjoyable life should be paused for 'needs that are more pressing'. This temporality presumes a progress of survival $\rightarrow$ liveable and only some will be able to undertake this movement.

This moving to the possibility of liveability was also linked to legislative changes (see Chapter 3):

Lucy: When I'm thinking about liveable as opposed to bearable, I mean people are always saying like, 'Oh well things are so much better than they were ten years ago, twenty years ago, da-da-da'. I understand the importance of knowing the past, but the point is that we need to move on to the next thing. So like, whereas ten years ago, it might just be okay for your workplace not to fire you for being LGBT, now we can move on to the next step which is to make it comfortable and kind of an easy life. To the point of which if you're LGBT, your life experience is unaltered in terms of your access to a good life, basically, and I think that's what you're always supposed to be striving towards.

(Project Workshop, England)

Lucy points to the complexities that we further explore and complicate in this section, namely the relationship between living and surviving.

In particular, we contest the duality of and movement between living and surviving/বেঁচে থাকা এবং টিকে থাকা (*benche thaka ebong tike thaka*/to live and to survive). We do this to contest the linearity of survival/living duality and the normative temporalities that this can assume (for example, that 'it gets better' for LGBTQ people as they age, see Goltz, 2013). Instead, we conceptualize survival and liveability as co-constitutive realities that can refuse hierarchization that presume particular temporal associations. Namely, we contest presumptions that underpin understandings of 'hierarchies of needs', namely that the 'basics' of survival need to be in place before the possibilities of a liveable life can be achieved. Our participants' framing of the concepts in conversation with Butler's work prompted us to consider how liveability is intimately linked to survival in a non-dichotomous way.

Our participants in India raised the non-dichotomous aspects of living and surviving through efforts to persist through violence and achieve 'a life worth living'. Participants were explicitly asked to reflect on the difference between বেঁচে থাকা (*benche thaka*/to live) and টিকে থাকা (*tike thaka*/to survive). Their responses contested the dichotomization of what constitutes living and surviving, pointing to how the two are interconnected, continuous and may define one's being together rather than being separated:

> Group discussion summary: Is surviving and living necessarily oppositional? Living means sometimes good, and surviving means sometimes negative? So we [the discussion group present] have some turmoil with these assumptions. And we started to ask ourselves what exactly we understand by these two phrases/words. And one thing we three realised is that we are confused. We think of it as a crisscrossing between living and surviving. But I don't know really how to differentiate this matter. That itself is unclear. Because every day we have to face challenges to survive, and we are surviving because we're living or are we living, therefore, we are surviving? So facing these challenges-to

both live and survive, we are unable to think of them as watertight compartments. I think liveability is about aspiration, a reminder to help me come out and overcome bad situations. That reminder is my will to live. But if I don't have a reminder and my life just continues as it is, just waking up, eating, sleeping, office, studies, then life becomes only about surviving. My drive, my reminder to stay alive, is liveability for me.

(Project Workshop, India)

The flows and links between living and surviving are apparent in this narrative. The group discussant speaks of the 'crisscrossing between living and surviving', refusing to render these hierarchical or differentiated 'watertight compartments'. Liveability allows for aspiration, however, which we engage with more in the next section. Dwelling on the word 'reminder' in temporal terms, we may understand the 'reminder of something' to mean that which once relegated to the outside of straight time now seeks to create a life outside that order (Munoz, 2009). Suppose life has to be something more than 'just waking up, eating, sleeping, office, studies'; in that case, liveability unfixes what Munoz terms 'straight time'. For us this means liveability connects it with surviving and preparing oneself in the present for something more beyond this time, and normative temporalities. Such temporal disruptions contest the linearity of survival and its existence before liveability queering the straightness, the linearity of these. Vaibhavi, when asked how she understands টিকে থাকা (*tike thaka*/to survive), said:

The water is flowing, the water is flowing downstream, and I have to swim upstream if I have to live. It's like swimming upstream. I have to reach the topside, and I am struggling, but if I fail, I will die. To live, to swim upstream, I have to anchor myself in something, or I have to look for something else to flow in the opposite direction. That I am flowing upstream, this is survival.

(In-depth interview, India)

Vaibhavi's powerful imagery of swimming upstream swept aside the temporal binary between surviving and living, pushing us to look at the efforts to survive as a form of living. The anchor points of such survival were situated by our participants in friendships, partnerships, ideas and collectives, which provide some security and comfort in the attempts to survive. For Vaibhavi, she told us that her 'mainstream friends' and her partner were anchorings. The former required fewer efforts than the latter because establishing herself with her partner in her wider social circle needed more struggle, given she resided in a semi-urban area. When asked if this meant that living was positive and surviving was negative, she said:

> No, no. I enjoy both; I feel I can balance both. But one requires more struggle and the other less. Living requires less struggle, and surviving is that which requires more struggle. When I am flowing with the stream, it requires less struggle. When I am flowing upstream, then it is survival.
>
> (In-depth interview, India)

Further complicating a simple linear hierarchy and normative temporality between surviving and living, some positioned living as the prerequisite of surviving. This reverses the presumed hierarchies of needs, as Akanksha explained:

> I think somewhere down the line, surviving is proving to myself that I am alive. I am saying that I have felt alive all my life. I would say I am just surviving when in order to be alive, I have to. When I lose them all, when the ingredients that make up my life are lacking, I say that's when I am surviving. As far as I understand, I am not comparing my present self with my past self, and it's all my sensibilities, intelligence and efficiency coming together to make me alive.
>
> (In-depth interview, India)

Refusing past/present as comparisons that allow for survival/living, Akanksha queers any linear temporal sensibility of living and surviving across her life course. She refuses to delineate as it is their 'all coming together' (to make it 'better'). Akanksha also disrupts associations of living as positive and surviving as unfavourable. Srabasti, in wanting to insert some 'humility' in the concept of living, helped us to 'release' surviving from any negative connotation, saying:

> There's not much difference between the two, although I am not trying to be a pessimist. I am surviving well. I am not demeaning the phrase, but if you consider, surviving is kind of living then.
> (In-depth interview, India)

Surviving is for Srabasti living, and both are key to feeling alive. For her, there is 'not much difference between the two'. They are interlocked, such that one needs to survive to live, and in turn, one needs at least the hope of living to survive. Not identifying survival with negativity and living with positivity and a normative idea of happiness (McGlynn, Browne et al., 2020) came up with several participants. They suggested that one needs to survive to live and that surviving is a necessary component of living, and the struggle involved in that process of survival translates to living, breathing with and through the odds.

If we are to dismantle the term, odds was not used as a generic category but was used in different ways to talk about individual and collective obstacles related to racism, economic stability, workplace discrimination, public spaces, violence at home and on the streets. Dharam and Jacques, two participants in a project workshop in England, suggested:

> Dharam: I mean, in relation to what doesn't make life liveable, as a gay South Asian Sikh man, I've come across some different types of prejudice and discrimination in different ways, shapes and forms. I know looking at some of the previous ones from previous workshops, they've put family in what makes life liveable, whilst I've put it in it doesn't make life liveable.

Jacques: That [name of city] the BME community's probably around about fifty per cent of the population of the city. That's not reflected on the LGBT scene at all. There are black and minority ethnic people on the scene, but it's predominantly white. I think for a lot of LGBT BME people, they're still terribly isolated in this city, and services for them are very few and far between, and the Local Authorities don't want to embrace that. They find it too difficult. One of the things about my life, one of the sort of drawbacks of living in [name of city], is what I'd like to see improved is the lip-service that's given by the City Council, a Labour-run council, a majority Labour council. It's solid Labour apart from one or two other party councillors. And being a Labour voter myself, but the city makes a big song and dance about the diversity of this city, which I think it should do, except that that emphasis is always on ethnicity and faith. The other strands, particularly sexuality, aren't embraced on the same level as ethnicity and faith, and there's an uncomfortableness with it, and it's the elephant in the room with the local politics here that because of I think the ethnic and faith make up of this city and the perception that they are sort of Labour voters, the councillors do not want to necessarily embrace LGBT issues regarding the services that they provide or lack of because they think it's a vote loser. My run-ins with the City Council I find very frustrating. I mean, they've only recently in the past couple of years, and I had a meeting with them, and the Deputy Mayor suggested, you know- They're not even on the Stonewall Equality Index. This is a Labour-run council. They've never even applied for it. Well, the County Council, which is often Tory-run, have been for some years and have been scoring quite highly, which I think speaks volumes of the lack of wanting to embrace LGBT issues within the City Council, and that affects my life regarding the sort of services or lack of support or promotion of LGBT services in the city. There's also other issues about, especially around about sort of the lack of support for LGBT people

> from BME backgrounds. They're having nowhere to go. Totally isolated. Homophobia within their community, racism on the LGBT commercial scene. Completely isolated. Where do they go? Nowhere to go.
>
> (Project Workshop, England)

Hearing the words of persons such as Dharam and Jacques brings out the complex intersectionalities and interplay between family, community, faith, ethnicity, race, local political dynamics and place. What is needed for life to become life, to become 'culturally viable' (Butler, 1993), is more than mere existence. Pointing to sites for ethico-political engagement and intervention, Jacques argues there is 'a big song and dance about the diversity of the city' in ways that emphasize faith/ethnicity but not LGBT 'issues' which are seen as a 'vote loser' (implying that racialized and faith communities are inherently anti-LGBT). Support for one group is seen to negate engagement with another.

There is a struggle in processes of survival-living, breathing with and through heteronormative power relations that constitute everyday lives (see Chapter 3). In the words of Ipshita:

> When you are backed into a corner, then you simply realize certain things. I will have to overcome this, and there are people around me who are ready to help me out. They are pulling me upwards. That is the sign, one sign, and a person is bound to fight back if they have even a tiny bit of will to live. It happened to me.
>
> (In-depth interview, India)

Ipshita locates liveability in struggle and solidarity with others. Liveability can mean being ready to 'fight back' while others are 'pulling me upwards'. This connects the individual struggle to a collective, wherein others are engaged and linked through the fightbacks. Even during their individually unique difficult times, participants talked about how a certain stubbornness and obstinacy

Figure 4 England Project Workshop. Image: Authors' Own.

to live, to get out of those difficulties in relation to others made life worth living (McGlynn et al., 2020). This stubbornness is in the will to not only live but live a life worth living. We were struck by Harriet discussing Figure 4:

> If you imagine a kind of filigree type sphere with a very bright light inside and cast shadows, and these are the shapes of the shadows that it's casting, because of the casing around whatever it is that I truly am, not only is the light dappled in some way that comes out of me. That's my identity, but also what I see projected on the walls are these shadows that I think are outside of me, but they only exist because of the prism, if you like, not really a prism but of the thing through which the light has to shine. And I think, 'Oh. There are these things in the world. How interesting', but all they are is a result of me not being aware of who I truly am. They can be very interesting and very beautiful. Like mountains and trees and

wolves, dogs, clouds and people. They can also be menacing. I can weave a story with them. Lovely stories or sad and painful ones.

(Project Workshop, England)

Invited to show a 'liveable life' in whatever way she chose, Harriet produced an illustration (Figure 4.1) in which even apparently external phenomena which are 'menacing', 'sad' or 'painful' emerge from her-self. These co-exist with 'interesting', 'very beautiful' and 'lovely' so that both the positive and negative phenomena are ultimately products of the 'filigree' of Harriet's liveable life. We take her illustration and her words to contend that living and surviving co-weave and intersect to form a non-linear and multiple states of being that could be both enabling and oppressive, together and separately varying over time/space/lifecoures.

Participants in India and England thus interpreted living and surviving in unique and creative ways, and sometimes the same term came out with entirely different meanings in different discussions. For instance, the terms 'alive' and 'living' at times signified the technical state of biological life (and survival at a base level) and at other times were meant to understand being in a state of mental, emotional, political wellness and happiness. The term 'surviving' was used to indicate barely existing and, at other times, hinted at the struggle and pain one endures to make life worth living (Browne et al., 2021). Survival, in other words, does not depart from living but can be used in a generative sense to mark the emergence of what may come rather than as something that deters the process of living.

Developing from Butler's (2015) conceptualization of the relationship between living and surviving, she rethinks her understanding of life as more than survival. As Butler contends, there cannot be a singular understanding of a liveable life; the state of survival is linked to conditions of precarity, a politically induced condition that is graded and historically specific. When animated with the words of our participants, survival comes alive as something else, which, while tied to particular experiences of precarity, is also a condition for liveability. To survive then points to an active condition – which can mean a struggle against odds, against base survival that itself may constitute a life worth living. Survival and living cannot be delineated or temporally assumed. Our participants contest any framing of living and surviving as dichotomous. The relationships between living and surviving are complex and reworked. Setting aside the variability of words used, it was thus fairly clear to us that life is ≠ to living, liveability, and life is ≠ to surviving, unliveability. This allows us to push the contours of liveability as a condition that is constituted only partially through survival, through its limits, and towards intersecting interdependences and access to resources. The struggle for a possible life can mean an awareness of the limitations of what is taken for granted to survive. An understanding of survival with the potential of living can seek to push normative boundaries in creating the realms of potential lives.

The normative and non-normative/ নিয়মতান্ত্রিক এবং নিয়মবিরোধী (*Niyomtantrik ebong niyombirodhee*)

There is a vigorous and ongoing discussion of the normative and non-normative in queer and sexuality studies, wherein an interpellation of the normative is deliberately done to critique the power relations that reconstitute sex, gender and sexuality. Normativity, understood with the concept of 'heterosexual matrix' (Butler, 1990),[1] signals rules, codes and scripts that lays down how a person ought to/should live. This is not ahistorical and is shaped by the colonial and postcolonial histories of nations.[2] Having said that, at the level of the individual, it is lived through repetitive and normalized prescriptions and proscriptions that guide social interaction, frame morally appropriate behaviour and set substantive life goals. All of this takes on a naturalized form through repetition and stabilization, which, when transgressed, is met with violation and violence. With Butler's work, we understand this as 'normative violence', i.e. a process through which gender and sex appear and solidify to form grids of intelligibility within which subjects are created and sorted in ahistorical ways, with both discursive and material effects (1990, 1993). Thinking with LGBTQ identifying bodies, normativity then is intricately linked to violation. The effort to be and become occurs through an encounter with the limits of the intelligible grid, historically shaped through intersecting oppressive systems of race, caste, class, ability, religion and location. Non-normativity then is a set of expressions, identities, behaviours, practices that emerge through the encounter with the normative, otherwise rendered unintelligible, invisibilized and silenced in historically specific ways. In this sense, it is not diametrically opposite to normativity but is constitutive of the normative. Where normativity and non-normativity are seen to co-constitute each other, then the moment of being and the process of becoming intelligible (and subjectification) and visible can be considered through liveability. Alternatively, the lives of LGBTQ identifying people can be considered non-normative and therefore liveable.

Chapter 3 underscored that liveability is not necessarily equal to normative happiness (see also McGlynn et al., 2020), and as we argued above, it is intimately connected with efforts to survive. An encounter with normative violence is part of this survival process and yet is also not divorced from what is considered a liveable life. Having said that, a non-normative being (understood as a person who has been rendered unintelligible, invisibilized and silenced) may stake a claim to living-surviving and surviving-living through the very norms and resources that have used them to keep the normative grid intact, with profound symbolic and material effects. Hence, in the narratives of liveability and what is not liveable, we have listened to aspirations, ambitions, expectations, anxieties that may seem to mimic the normative. Yet, such a reading is also reductive, and when placed in its context, such narratives can speak to underlying structures of violence. Consider the following words of Appy:

> I used to think that if I got married, I would not feel anything for other women. I could not cope with the fact that I could not find a suitable woman. Perhaps staying with a man would not be the best course, but at least it would have distracted me from the ongoing crisis [of not finding a stable relationship with a woman]. It [wanting to marry] was the easy way out. I did not want to fight. I was not fine, why I should care for others; why I should choose something that always hurt me; let me stay mediocre.
>
> (In-depth interview, India)

The security of a straight life with its apparent conjugal comfort and stability allows for a mediocrity that can distract from unapproved desires and the potential negative consequences of non-normative relationships. The fears of finding 'suitable' partners, not wanting to fight, did not make Appy 'fine', but it holds a promise of an 'easier life' without having to engage in external fights. Marriage as a tried and tested method with its given structure promised advantages and apparent social security. For Appy, that is survival 'that does not hurt', even though the marriage might. Thus, liveability can take on meaning in relation to the normative institution of marriage, a hegemonic frame that several participants spoke of negotiating. Navigating the material reality of heterosexual marriage, particularly its intense pressure for a non-normative person assigned gender female at birth, can be built into the search for a liveable life. Those cis, lesbian and bisexual LB identifying women interviewed in India calibrated and referenced their lives in connection to the marriage institution. Some were clearly saying they would be unable to marry a man, while others said they were open to the idea, as it's a secure option. At the same time, navigating the pressures of marriage for persons assigned gender female at birth is done through strategizing, such as rejecting prospective grooms for marriage and stalling time until one can move out of one's home either by getting a job or relocating to another place for educational pursuits. This meant they could buy time and make their own decisions regarding pursuing an academic degree programme or how they wanted to live their lives. In almost all instances, the latter meant living with their partners, which for Appy was part of the issue, what does one do when 'a suitable woman' is not 'found'?

The pressure to marry was commonly shared by many Indian participants, either because the family expects it or because it is thought of as the only route to a secure and stable life. A participant explained:

> I want a job now. I would tell them [family] after completing my MSc, I am trying to maintain the peace before that.
>
> (Project Workshop, India)

Given the existing 'order of being' (Butler, 2004a), Appy's sharing does not comfortably fit the normative/non-normative binary. What Appy can do, what she can be, how she can be are dependent on where and how she can strategize, to survive and make her life one that she sees as a life worth living.

The desire to live a 'normal life' is not necessarily tied to the advancement of equalities legislation and the legal possibilities of same-sex marriage, as the English work showed:

> Mel: As a person challenging norms knowingly and sometimes unknowingly, I had always faced antagonism. There was a time when I felt so tired fighting shadow demons; I tried to live a 'normal' life, straight life. I wanted to be accepted and appreciated by people who matter to me; I thought that will make my life liveable because they will be happy, and seeing them happy, I will also feel happy. But it did not happen, I was

never a straight person, and people who matter to me could not accept me the way I am. It created havoc in their lives and in my life as well, as our lives were connected to each other, liveabilities and happiness were connected. Or so I thought. Today I believe in my own life, queer or straight, crooked or simple, I believe in myself. I want to be appreciated, but I know even if people who matter to me do not appreciate me, my life will remain important for me. It is liveable because I choose to make it so.

(Project Workshop, England)

The choice to make life liveable in the face of normative straight lives means that some will never 'appreciate' or accept this. The choice to live without acceptance and appreciation makes life liveable outside the boundaries of normative happiness (Ahmed, 2007). As Sheila succinctly argues:

Hilary: My life will be more liveable if I conform to society's norms when I'm out on the street, and I'm out in the world. Everybody else around me is going to react to me in a way that makes things more liveable, but internally perhaps there's going to be more conflict. So that's going to be less liveable. So there's different types of liveability going on there.

(Project Workshop, England)

For Sheila, liveable lives can be created through the reactions of others and broader societal normativities. These can conflict with the self, desires and aspirations that work against such normativities and make life less liveable. Thus normativities act against liveabilities by both conforming to them and contesting them.

Engagement with liveability inevitably takes us through different voices and varied living practices that push us to question the neat binary between the normative/non-normative, including its political implications. While following the norm of (heterosexual) marriage and non-disclosure may seem normative and devoid of political possibilities as it can be associated with assimilation and conforming with norms, our work points to the need to explore the contextual conditions that do not allow a living otherwise. Marriage (and partnering) pressures, having to fit specific standards, the insecurities of ageing figure into the routes one takes to achieve a life worth living and how one engages with the normativities that constitute everyday life. The line between normativity/non-normativity is thus very slippery. Yet, critiques of normativities may not account for the differential access to non-normative ways of living. Becoming non-normative can be intricately tied to location, class, race, ethnicity and caste. In Figure 5, the phrase আমার বেঁচে থাকা (*amar benche thaka*/my living) including দুঃসাহসিক অভিযান (*duhsahosik abhijan*/daring adventure), আন্দোলন (*andolon*/movement), ভালবাসা (*bhalobasa*/love), সৃষ্টি (*srishti*/creation), আনন্দ (*anondo*/happiness), স্বাধীনতা (*swadhinata*/freedom) is perhaps a mix of reality and aspirations. None of these

Figure 5 Project Workshop, Kolkata.

offers the entirety of a person's being and can be read as a call to collectively imagine what might be possible if life were liveable on one's own terms.

One's terms, however, are located within normative structures. In another project workshop, which consisted of several trans* participants from small towns and semi-urban areas in West Bengal, we can see the effort to secure economic survival and get access to formal education:

> Yes, when I was young, my family's financial condition was weak. My father was a farmer, and he had suffered from some mental illness which further exacerbated our problems. I live in a remote area, not many educated people around, and it's almost a miracle that I have completed my Master's degree with that background. I knew I had to change things around no matter what. I had to overcome too many adversities; there had been days when I had nothing to eat and still went to school. The school paid for my education, all the fees and books. They helped me a lot. And when I was in class seven or eight, my father's mental problem degenerated, and our condition became worse. I had to stay at my maternal uncle's home nearby and continue my studies.
>
> (Project Workshop, India)

The struggle to secure one's food and livelihood can require engaging with 'normals' and even desiring normality that feels unattainable. As Dev explained:

> Like my dad goes to office, mingles with his friends, gets promoted, my dad has always been my role model. I have seen myself just like he goes to office and he is respected in his office; I also see myself going to the corporate world, coming back home and frankly, regarding family, I don't think about it because I do not know how [to get to that life]. Suppose I love a girl, and that girl loves me. After that, if I am in a relationship, of course, I will tell her [that I am a transman], I don't know how she will react, and I totally hate

rejection, so I do not know if I want to start a family or not; maybe if someday I get someone who can accept me as who I am maybe I will start, maybe I won't. I don't know about it yet.

(In-depth interview, India)

When the line between normativity and non-normativity is slippery, then liveability can be understood as a conditional and contingent state that has the potential to both reproduce (through mimicry) and upset the normalizing norm. Liveability can be a normative condition that individuals and groups can aim to attain, with or without legal reforms. The porous boundary between the normative and non-normative in our data augments consideration of the robust critiques of homonormativities (Duggan, 2002; Warner, 1991), normalizations and the exclusions that legislative changes have brought about, including the prioritization of monogamous marriage-like relationships and same-sex marriage (Warner, 1999a, 1999b; Wilkinson, 2012, 2020), the commodification of LGBTQ lives (Duggan, 2002; O'Brien, 2008; Sears, 2005), and the assimilationist politics of LGBTQ liberal agendas, including its racialized, classed and casteist manifestations (Brown & Borisa, 2021; Ponniah & Tamalapakula, 2020; Richardson, 2005; Sircar, 2021; Sircar & Jain, 2017).

Our work suggests that sticking to critiques of normalizations, while essential, also has limitations. The call to be political – in academic critiques of normalizations – while well taken, can at times hide the subtleties of existence, including complex alliances with blood-related kins, debilitating instances of prejudice in the workplace and public spaces, emotional fragility due to lack of access to a support network outside of blood and marriage, all of which amount to micro-injuries in the everyday, which can have life-altering consequences, including devastation and death. Liveability, as a normative condition to sustain life, can render visible these subtleties and micro-injuries located in the slippery slopes of the normative/the non-normative, sometimes which are so proximal and banal that they become invisibilized in our rush to find the political as an instant intention. Thus, while there is a need for virulent critiques of a standardized way of living and activisms that seek to achieve a collective vision of a non-liberal understanding of equality and change, there is a need also to explore becoming normal and those who had no interest in activist collectives at all. Browne and Bakshi, drawing from Sedgewick (2003) and Halberstam (2011: 1), remind us, one can get lost in the 'ubiquitousness of critique, leading to hopelessness' and in 'cynical resignation' (2013: 188–9) here; our focus on the rich texture of everyday experiences turns us now to the place of ordinariness, alongside other political forms.

The ordinary and the everyday/সাধারণ আর গতানুগতিক (*sadharon ar gotanugotik*)

> Akshara: I am a lesbian; I can say that as a human being, I am doing alright in this society, although as a lesbian, I am not. Social, relational, familial problems are faced by me. Along with my own family pressures I need to also handle my partner's family pressure. A normal, ordinary life is not something we live, so I am kind of surviving in a way.
> (In-depth interview, India)

> Alex: I think it's important that we kind of have our own communities, but hopefully, for our future, that will become less and less necessary, and I think that's what being liveable is. It is like we kind of need these kind of safe pockets now, and we need the support of our community now, but eventually…
> (Project Workshop, England)

We begin this section with quotes that open up our discussions of the pursuit of ordinary lives that allow for more than survival and 'safe pockets'. Instead, these quotes speak to seeking an everyday where relationships, desires and identities are 'something we live'. These do not require support or specific 'pockets' that are differentiated from the daily undertakings of life. They are ordinary but not necessarily normative. As we saw in Chapter 1, ordinariness can be equated with normativity and eradicating difference has been critiqued by those who worry about the conditionalities of making sexual difference not 'matter' (Richardson & Monro, 2012; Santos, 2013: 156). What we explore in this section is the quest for an ordinary life through explorations of liveable lives that are not confined to the normative. This detaches the normal from the ordinary and asks for consideration of the political implications of the normal in ways that do not assume normalization.

The political and social effort to achieve a liveable life happens within the everyday through aspirations, expectations and survival tactics that are often ordinary, trite, mundane. The lack of ordinariness can be seen through the subtle contestations of heteronormativities (Chapter 3). It can differentiate bearable from liveable through the slow and repeated differentiation from normal. As Dale said:

> Bearable is, I would say, those kind of subtle homophobic comments that you get that sort of hard to describe and feels like slowly your self-esteem is being pelted with pebbles. It's that kind of; I think that's the difference between liveable and bearable for me.
> (Project Workshop, England)

Dale's description of being 'pelted with pebbles' speaks to the repeated small and often overlooked ways in which difference is established and felt problematic. Let's look at the normative commitment to equal access to material resources required to sustain a life. The process of self-identification that borrows from the heteronormative matrix to become recognizable and the need to go beyond racial discrimination and trans-negativity, then the quest for ordinariness cannot be easily folded into the normative and the non-normative in binary terms. Instead, what seems banal has an ethical sensibility and a political implication:

> I'm not doing well. I'm a transgender person, and the daily harassment and discrimination we face are multiple. There are

limited facilities and resources for transpersons. Anyone who cannot fit into the neat boxes of 'ladies' and 'gentlemen' is marked as different for life.

(Project Workshop, India)

Sylvia in England spoke of withdrawing from the world; the project workshop she attended was one of the only times she had ventured into LGBTQ spaces. Her story speaks to reactions to difference that is felt as unsafe, which does not allow for a liveable life but enables her to feel safe.

> Sylvia: I think it's the little things that make life liveable. It's the not having to endure the little snide remarks and being treated with just courtesy and respect. I think it's not so much happy as safe. You don't want to hurt anyone, and you don't want to be hurt, you know, it's all this. It just becomes too much of a big deal if you put it off for too long, and like I said, I didn't really plan to put it off [laughs] as I had done for quite a long period. It became a big deal for me.
> KB: When you get yourself into that corner almost, it's hard then to-
> Sylvia: It's hard to come out of it. That's true.
> KB: Unless you're really enjoying it.
> Sylvia: But there are advantages to the corner as well [laughs].
> KB: What are the advantages?
> Sylvia: Well, like I said. You don't get hurt. You don't go through the dramas and the traumas [laughter] or heartbreak or the guilt of breaking someone else's heart. You avoid all of that stuff, but yeah, it's not really living. I know what you're saying. It's not really. You don't feel any joy either. You're just kind of –
> Kath: Surviving.
> Sylvia: Yeah. Just kind of flat-lining [laughter]. But it's safe.

(Project Workshop, England)

Where differences are felt unsafe, it can limit lives restricting happiness and liveability. Sylvia recognized the safety of her metaphorical corner, but also its limitations. Avoiding the world in order to not hurt or be hurt meant 'not really living'. Living can be unintentionally put off, its safe but 'flat lining'.

Reactions to feelings of lacking safety can draw on forms of privilege to negotiate everyday lives and carve out spaces, as Preet explains:

> So I am forcing to change myself, and people are not open enough to accept that. Even if I go through SRS [sex reassignment surgery], grow a beard and change my identity, take up a man's name, the society still would not accept me; people would point me out as a freak who wanted to be a man. I belong to a mostly uneducated neighbourhood, so coming from that place, I tried to change myself. I did not want to limit my identity there, I tried, and now people communicate with me, not out of fear of the unknown, but with an understanding that this person is a bit different; an educated person with a big job, so they should watch themselves before they make a fool out of themselves while talking to me.
> (In-depth interview, India)

Preet recognizes the reactions to difference and those who 'would point me out as a freak' and hints at the aspiration for a society that would accept. Deploying educational privilege to offset a 'fear of the unknown' speaks to the desire to be known and accepted. It also speaks to the transience of liveabilities that move over life courses, refusing fixity. Thus, suggesting that mobilities and challenges as liveabilities and the privileges accrued to deal with those who 'would not accept me' swell and contract. As Georgina said:

> I guess I also think like having told you about times when it feels less liveable, and the times when it felt most liveable, even if I'm romanticising all of that now, it does feel like it's somehow capturing some kind of ebb and flow of my life, that sometimes I feel like something is like swelling and something is really- It feels really good and then other times it's like contracting, and it feels, I don't know, somehow much more closed-in, less connected.
> (Project Workshop, England)

These ebbs and flows further engage with the temporalities of lives that can be liveable and less or not liveable within and beyond the strict dictates of 'basic needs' and survival. Such queer temporalities are not only queer heteronormative trajectories; they also offer critical insights into how difference feels to live with, in and through the flows of everyday lives.

A self-identified trans-heterosexual cis-man offered us an insight into the ebbs and flows of the journeys and mobilities of self-recognition which afford happiness, through difference from heteronorms:

10–20 years:
-First time falling in love with a girl and getting physically intimate. Going from school to college and then finally beginning to earn
-I'm in my boy-hood

21–30 years:
-Finding true love, having a great time romancing, and finally getting married
-College-sweetheart, got married at Dakshineshwar Mandir[3]
-My own business
-I'm a man

31–40:
-Leaving my business and joining a job
-Going to Sappho and understanding more about myself
-Becoming a member of Sappho, finding many friends, and staying mentally happy
-I am mentally a man, but according to my body, I am an F/M man

41–42:
-I am happy till now, with my family and Sappho, without a wife.
-Even now, both physically and psychologically, I am 22 years of age

-I am a trans-heterosexual-cis-man – Till now, I'm happy (Project Workshop, India)

When the everyday, including its place-based manifestations, is experienced as fragile, oppressive and discriminatory, an orientation towards ordinariness can be political. Figure 6, produced by an anonymous participant in a project workshop in Kolkata, juxtaposes several ordinary everyday objects with the Bangla words নীতি (*neeti*/values, morals), প্রতিবাদ (*protibad*/protest), আন্দোলন (*andolon*/movement), among others. This speaks to how ordinary objects can be interpellated with meaning that seeks to counter the heteronorms in the everyday. নীতি (*neeti*/values, morals), প্রতিবাদ (*protibad*/protest) and আন্দোলন (*andolon*/movement) are thus not outside the everyday, but embedded within the mundane, the familiar, the ordinary. The value of these words resides precisely in the ordinary relationships through which one orders the everyday, some of which, while seemingly assimilationist, requires adherence to the specific norms

Figure 6 India Workshop.

of a place. This both can be particular to particular people and is also part of a collective, where activism thrives in the everyday, to make lives liveable:

> For me, বেঁচে থাকা (*benche thaka*/to live, living) is collectivity; staying with a group is being connected. Even if one person is unhappy, then it affects the group, and this connection is important to my living. Movement is a part of my living, like the women's movement I'm already associated with and simultaneously my Sappho friends and our movement here. Every day, not a single moment of the day, I am away from the movement, beginning with using public transport for going to office, and I've kept a point here – living is going against mainstream heteropatriarchal framework.
>
> (Project Workshop, India)

নীতি (*neeti*/values, morals), প্রতিবাদ (*protibad*/protest) and আন্দোলন (*andolon*/movement) are woven into the ordinary particularities of living and surviving with a collective, and understanding difference as political. An ordinary concern for the other, to be able to be useful to the other, thus becomes meaningful in the everyday across axes of difference that connect the individual to the collective and the collective to the individual:

> বেঁচে থাকা (*benche thaka*/to live, living) is being able to support others, which is, of course [means] people from the community but also people in general in my case. For example, Addy was trying to change his gender in his passport, for which he had to speak to Paresh and look through the internet. So when I was talking to Paresh for the first time on Facebook chat, I felt that my connecting with Paresh, talking to him in English, trying to help Addy – and if I didn't join Sappho in 2009, then I wouldn't have been able to do any of this. Along with this, the Internet and the English language are both tools-these made me feel that I was living in a particular way.
>
> (Project Workshop, India)

Conclusion

> Charlie: It [Liveability] doesn't imply extremes about either no life being completely wonderful or completely shit, you know, like isn't it always to do with a process of negotiating and trying to tip the balance [laughter] in favour of something more liveable rather than less liveable. It feels like a way of thinking that is realistic, perhaps. I don't expect life to be all flowers and sunshine and bloody wonderful. I'm okay with it being boring sometimes, and I'm okay with it being shit sometimes a bit. I kind of wouldn't want it to be like that all the time, but you know. So I do like the concept.
>
> (Project Workshop, England)

When placed in the ordinary and the everyday, liveability reworks a straightforward correlation between the normal, normative and normalization, refusing to fix any of these in one place or time. This does not make liveability outside critique, nor does it exist in stark distinction to critiques of normalizations, but allows it to breathe as a state of being in the world, with the self and the bodies of others, in numerous unspecifiable ways. The multiple nature of what constitutes a liveable life shows the importance of multiple liveabilities that do not differentiate or hierarchize survival and living. Liveability cannot be predicted or defined in advance but can be given space or acquired to be created and enhanced.

The desire for ordinariness pays heed to the exhaustion that some can feel in constantly occupying or being placed in other positionings where difference is not accepted and lives made less liveable through marginalizations and exclusions (Ahmed, 2014). The role played by struggles, challenges and fights in how participants understood and expressed this complicated and multidirectional interplay between living and surviving/বেঁচে থাকা এবং টিকে থাকা (*benche thaka ebong tike thaka*/to live and to survive), the normative and non-normative/

নিয়মতান্ত্রিক এবং নিয়মবিরোধী (*Niyomtantrik ebong niyombirodhee*) and the ordinary and the everyday/সাধারণ আর গতানুগতিক (*sadharon ar gotanugotik*), including attendant material and discursive realities – surviving and living. Thus all 'good'/'positive' feelings do not equate to 'what makes a life liveable', and all 'unwell/bad' things do not always make life unliveable. Liveabilities cannot just incorporate all the happy things that have been a part of a life or all the good things that one desires for a future; instead, it ebbs and flows, refusing directionalities. Moreover, the struggle for a liveable life is to be cognizant of the limitations of what is given, and awareness of constraints is to push those limitations to create what is, and might be, possible.

The aspirations, anxieties, need for security can be read as how the desire for the ordinary pushes through the normalized everyday and embodied realities of violence and discrimination while simultaneously interpellating a future yet to arrive. Yet, liveability, where it encompasses efforts to work towards ordinary, does not hold a political potential, but in interactional, relational and placed-based settings inhabits a possibility of transfiguring existing patterns of living and conceptions of place. A state of liveability, informed through individual and collective spaces in place, can create new norms with resultant exclusions but also has the potential to create liveabilities. When tilting towards normalizations, such normative conditions must be and are resisted. Thus the work of activisms can seek to create 'possibilities of ordinariness' (Browne & Bakshi, 2013) that do not become normalized. The next chapter explores the potentials and limitations of striving for ordinariness through street theatre.

5

Performing liveabilities in Kolkata and Brighton: Creating new commonplaces

Introduction

The key to conceptualizing liveable lives is its potential for something else, something more liveable. There is an imagination, and indeed an excitement, around performing liveabilities. This chapter links the epistemological underpinnings of liveability to its performance and possibilities of other forms of ordinariness, which we conceptualize through a politics of commonplace. In conversation with geographies of sexualities literature that explores the possibilities of pride and marches as transforming heteronormative spaces (Bell & Valentine, 1995; Browne, 2007b; Johnston, 2007), we focus on street theatre workshops and performances in Kolkata and Brighton as a means of generating new possibilities for everyday spaces for those who participate and onlookers. At the same time, we, along with our participants, perceived a momentary change in our lives in terms of being transported to an elsewhere that held rich potential for critical relationalities. Such relationality is key to the re-constitution of places (Browne & Bakshi, 2013; Hubbard, 2006) and illustrates the potential of street theatre to create an elsewhere in the here and now. To forge a spatial-conceptual linkage between the street theatre performances and pride events, we asked ourselves if our performances would fall into the normativities of commercialization, especially in Brighton.

Pride events are often discussed in terms of commercialization, pinkwashing and homonormativities (Conway, 2021; Lamusse, 2016; Kates & Belk, 2001), but at the same time, their potentials are also well recognized (Browne & Bakshi, 2013; Di Feliciantonio, 2016; Kenttamaa Squires, 2019). These studies refuse a simplistic reading of diverse pride events and explore pride's problematic and transformative potentials beyond juridical equality measures. Further, street theatre performances in Kolkata are tied to a layered history of place, politics and critique.[1] A mode of politico-cultural activism, street theatre as a form of protest work has been part of the life of Kolkata as well as historically oppressed groups in several Indian contexts. Therefore, we are interested in the possibilities of working with relationalities that can feel fixed through discussions that lead to performances in place.

Rather than engaging with the possibilities and potentials of street theatre as an art form or change that can be measured across an extended period of time, in this chapter, our focus instead is on transnational connections that seek to create change momentarily in place in ways that interrupt everyday spaces for a short period. We outline the doing (methodological) and knowing (epistemological) underpinnings of our use and interpretations of street theatre. Following this, in one section after another, we present empirical vignettes, including the performance and workshop scripts[2] to selectively describe the performances in Kolkata and Brighton.[3] The chapter concludes with possibilities, connections and placing of street theatre performances in momentary social change within and beyond the discourse of equalities and rights. Overall, this chapter delineates the performative aspects of liveability and the temporal possibilities and limitations of street theatre in place, placing sexual and gender politics in the here inhabited by street theatre performers and their onlookers.

Commonplace politics

The street theatre workshops and the performances in Kolkata and Brighton speak to a politics of creating difference as ordinary, but also as common to a place, and holding place 'in common'. In this case, the fleeting interference with the norms of public space sought to create new forms of ordinariness. Commonplace politics are necessary *because* some bodies, identities, relationships and practices remain 'out of place', excluded, marginalized and stigmatized (see Cresswell, 1997). Conversely, as we have shown throughout this book and others have extensively argued, being 'in place'/included via what is obtained through equalities legislation may also mean that LGBTQ identifying people continue to feel out of place in new sexual and gender landscapes (Browne & Bakshi, 2013a; Herek, 2002, 2009; Monro and Richardson, 2012; Moran, 2002; Taylor et al., 2012).

Commonplace has yet to be discussed in any depth. However, passing references are instructive. McCarter (2008), an architect, points to two valuable aspects of commonplace. The first is *the common* that 'underlies community that defines place and identity' (McCarter, 2008: 9), and the second is that which might be seen as a common in regularity, in the way that it is 'the *common sense* that orders everyday life' (McCarter, 2008: 9). Considering creating a common through community created through workshops seeks to address or at least highlight the common-sense norms that can structure place (Cresswell, 1997). This offers something other than the 'exceptional' or 'alternative' politics, such as pride, protest marches or other queer activisms that are deliberately opposed to homo/heteronorms. It moves beyond the binary of in place/out of place to think about what might be made common to a place through the notion of the commons.

The commons is frequently understood through 'common-pool resources' studies, which have modelled how to manage resources communally and sustainably (García-López, 2013; Ostrom, 1990). This field has been critiqued for its lack of explorations of power relations that are spatially specific; this is arguably addressed through a focus on political ecology (García-López, 2013). Relatedly the loss of the urban commons is often mourned where public space and land used 'in common' are increasingly privatized and regulated under neo-liberal regimes. However, as Harvey (2011: 105) argues:

> The commons is not ... something extant once about a time that has since been lost, but something that ... is continuously being produced.

Dawney (2013: 33) sees the commons as formed through *commoning*, the 'processes and practices of making worlds together'. For Dawney, then, commons are about the practices of commoning, rather than specific spaces, moving her away from 'the seemingly unstoppable forces of enclosure' (35). She focuses on small acts, such as picking up litter or looking after communal areas at work. Street theatre, considered as a politics of the commons, can involve practices that make people feel part of something and feel like they have collective stakes. This involves thinking about the material ways in which the common is produced that organize bodies so that a sense of shared life is enabled and fostered (Dawney, 2013). For the days of the workshops and performances, our shared and different lives occupied the here and the now to create a place in common. Conceptualizing street theatre through commoning thus allows for the possibilities of a place created through the processes and practices that form the workshops and performances.

Seeing commonplace as created through practices of commoning allows for an appreciation of commonality and what might be held in common – to create a commons of shared ideas, imaginations and resources, and also different ways of deliberately working with each other to create and ask for new social spaces. Sumita facilitated the workshops to actualize the creation of a temporary commons that allowed for LGBTQ identifying people to be in-place, who were once out-of-place. Further, they/we were not only 'in place' but also common to the place itself and with each other by creating liveability in performance. The performance in the chosen locations acted as a micro-spatial creation of new forms of commonplaces. In these places, the enactment of live theatre was done to make lives more liveable by interrupting the common sense of a place and momentarily creating a different space held in common between performers, and between performers and onlookers. Of course, as a performance, the street theatre enactments, because of their substantive matter, were inherently disruptive and out of place. Indeed they sought to intervene to change common-sense norms, if only fleetingly. The performances and workshops then exist as a paradox in seeking commonplace through disruptive enactments. The stories, games and songs that were created were a braid of the extraordinary and the ordinary, hence sometimes normative, and at other times existing as critique, but never a-political.

During workshops and street theatre performances, the places and neighbourhoods in Kolkata and Brighton were temporarily shared or inhabited in common and collectively created in ways that did not necessarily impose normative agendas. This returns us to place as a critical constituent of ordinariness and its potential. Becoming commonplace depends on the place (and time) where one might realize it or create it. It is not available to all, everywhere, all the time. Ordinariness and the possibilities of creating interventions and new commonplaces then are always spatially and temporally contingent, just as critiques of homo/heteronormativities need to account for their spatial and temporal manifestations (Brown & Browne, 2016). Practising commonplace can thus be seen as political, even as it strives for ordinariness.

Practising commons, doing street theatre

As the last section has indicated, the imagination of living and surviving as an LGBTQ identifying person and acting it out in the present with each other and connecting with the onlookers to create new commonplaces underlay our performances in Kolkata and Brighton. In the summer of 2015, we performed two street plays in Kolkata and Brighton that were the culmination of workshops in each city. Theatre workshops were conducted in Kolkata and Brighton before the performances, where scripts were developed in collaboration with the participants, rehearsals were undertaken, and the performances finalized. The workshops were used to gather information on how liveability is experienced, discussed and imagined, and as a modality of expressing a counter-discourse within contexts that either use or circumvent LGBTQ identifying lives for their gains. In this sense, it operated as an embodied methodology. Embodied methodologies are used to connect life stories, and praxis in processes of collective theorization (Fox, 2015), and scholars have drawn attention to its ability to capture the extra discursive, the sensory, the affective and fleshier aspects of research (Chadwick, 2017), and deployed it as a non-canonical and decolonizing move across academic and activist spaces (Nagar, 2019). We combined this with an understanding that theatre can be a productive methodological device to produce different kinds of knowledge for both participants and the research team. As Kaptani and Yuval-Davis suggested in their research on participatory theatre, it allows for an 'active embodiment of the narratives within a dialogical space created for action, reflection and "becoming"' (2008: 3). The idea of adopting the street theatre as a methodological device was suggested by Sumita, our activist partner in Sappho for Equality, who wrote the piece that started this chapter. Sumita's experience and interest with/in theatre dovetailed with our intention to engage with transformative performative possibilities inherent to reconstituting commonplaces. The question that drove us was 'how life can be made liveable?' and street theatre as a methodology offered to engage people in responding to the question practically.

As a mode of meaning-making, our workshops and street performances worked to delve into our knowledge of liveability via our bodies, stories that we created with the narratives shared from the project workshops and participants' lived experiences. Street theatres and the associated workshops allowed the dissemination of the research and a way of participating in making change through creating new forms in/common, however fleetingly, in the practices that create a place. We sought to emphatically interrupt public imaginations in the two cities and introduce a dialogue between our onlookers and us. The performances sought to spin out the political from the experiences of living and surviving, contextualizing the demands of our participants. We identified our ideas of 'liveabilities' during the workshops with the help of performing 'item numbers',[4] television adverts, short stories, games and silent tableaus. We then created performances that spoke to participants' experiences, the place we were in and the desires for lives that are more liveable.

We also bring embodied methodologies into conversation with our transnational participatory research and, in particular, move beyond comparative methods that consider one place (Brighton) as 'sorted' and the other (Kolkata) as 'failing'. The street performances were conceived as an alternative modality to have a conversation amongst ourselves, participants and onlookers about what makes life not/liveable with and beyond juridico-political measures (Chapter 3). The workshops and the performances were video-recorded and represented through the Liveable Lives film[5] made by filmmaker and Sappho for Equality member, Debalina. The creation of a film sought to extend the transnational reach of the street theatre process/methodology and offer other engagements and discussions, many of which cannot be known by us or those involved in the project (at the time of writing in

2021, the film has had over 4000 views). Even then, its existence may make something once uncommon more common. Our deployment of an embodied street theatre methodology moves between critical urban engagements and transnational interconnections and discussions exploring relationalities that are both in and of place and move between places creating new connections. We now turn to the narratives of the performances captured through the filmmaking process and within the material from the workshops, including our own experiences (Niharika participated in all the India workshops, and Kath attended all the UK workshops). We do so whilst exploring transnational connections in the narratives.

The experiences of street theatre's transformative potential centralize place in our structure and temporalities. Workshops and street theatre performances were first carried out in Kolkata and then Brighton. In the following paragraphs, we present select details from both the cities, of how they were created in form and content. This offers insights into the construction of the street play and the formation of the script for the performances. As the street theatre was, it is experimental, disconcerting and seeks practices that create commons without negating difference. This also recognizes our participants as essential team members to whom we brought our material and sought to reimagine other possibilities through building knowledge and practices together.

Performing liveabilities in Kolkata[6]

I Script My Script/আমার ভাষা আমার ভাষা[7]
Two steps ladders are used to set the scenes. In scene 1 they are used as two trees, scene 2 they are two sides of the public toilet, in scene 3 they are used as two houses, scene 4 one as the mental asylum, and other as the stretcher cum ECT[8] machine, scene 5 one is taken out and the other becomes the seat for IPC 377.

*A song was created as a crowd puller, using a musical form
গম্ভীরা/Gambheera.*[9]

মনে মনে ভাবব, ভেবে কাজ করব
মানুষকে অপমান করব না
সকল মানুষের সমান অধিকার
সেকথা ভুলতে পারব না।

মেয়েলি পুরুষ, পুরুষালি নারী
যেমন খুশি বাঁচতে পারি
সকল মানুষের সমান অধিকার
সেকথা ভুলতে পারব না।

সমকামী হোক বা রূপান্তরকামী
হিজড়া কোতি বা উভকামী
সকল মানুষের সমান অধিকার
সেকথা ভুলতে পারব না।

*Let us think, let us act
And let us make a solid pact
That we will not disregard anyone ...
You and I and we all have
Right to live and right to love
Equal rights for everyone ...*

*Butch girl or femme boy
Are you tough, are you coy
Equal rights for everyone ...*

*Lesbian, gay or bi
Trans, queer, are you shy
Equal rights for everyone ...*

Scene 1

Two participants are holding two branches with leaves on the step ladders as trees. Below Tree 1 sits a 'heterosexual couple', below Tree 2 sits a 'homosexual couple'. Both are engaged in different acts of 'romance'. Both couples are 'romancing' in a similar way.

One tea and one peanut vendor are hawking in the park. They are both making faces at the 'homosexual' couple. 'Homo case, 377, two girls in love' can be heard. The 'heterosexual' couple was also participating in the abuse. A crowd (public) collects and start chanting – 'dirty, pervert, sick, criminal, psycho, unnatural' – 'unnatural' is being repeated while they are pushed off-stage throwing 'stones' (made out of old newspapers and musk tapes) at them. This action is repeated in every scene.

The two trees come front-stage and one of them picks up a placard reading unnatural – asking the audience what it means through sign language. The other tree signals in a morose way that it doesn't know.

Chorus: 'গাছেরা বলেনা অস্বাভাবিক, আদালত কথা বলে, মানুষের কথা মানুষ বলেনা সমাজের মতে চলে' *(trees won't tell you what is unnatural, the court would direct you a human won't spare a moment for another, rather would listen to the society)*

Tree 1
Tree 2
Hetero-couple
Homo-couple
Peanut vendor
Tea seller
Public
Chorus

Scene 2

A public toilet – two persons sitting top of the ladders holding 'male (moustache)' and 'female (bindi)' signs. Two women wearing red dot on their foreheads (bindi) as sign of a female enter the stage and enter the 'female' section. One of them pays while the other doesn't. Gatekeeper (of the public toilet) stops the woman who was about to enter without payment; who ultimately gives money unwillingly. A man (with a moustache) hurriedly enters the 'male' toilet after paying. A trans-person (with bindi and moustache both) comes on stage, looks at the two signs (male-female), ponders for some time and decides to enter the 'male' section. The gatekeeper blocks the way and points at his bindi on his forehead, to which he shows his moustache. The 'man' comes out of the toilet in the meantime and the gatekeeper points to his moustache as an example of 'male'ness. A heated argument breaks out between them and the two women who had previously entered the toilets come out and support the transperson. The 'public' comes on-stage and starts abusing them and pushing them off-stage. Two people come down from the 'toilet', pick up a placard with the word pervert written. They both ask what it means and ultimately leave without an answer.

Chorus: বিকৃত তুমি, সমাজ বলেছে, সমাজ তো সব জানে, খুনি, ধর্ষক পার পেয়ে যায়, ভালবাসা হার মানে' *(you are a pervert, society tells you, society that knows all the murderer, the rapist can get away but the lover will go to jail)*

Woman 1
Woman 2
Transperson
Gatekeeper
Man
Public toilet (man and woman)
'Public'
Chorus

Scene 3

Two step ladders become two houses, two people on them as roof of two houses. Two sets of parents come out one after the other. One set of parents try to coax and cajole the girl to leave her lover, the other set of parents physically hurt their daughter and force them apart. They scream out 'ma, please don't hit me anymore … papa please let go of me.' In the commotion a gender-neutral person comes out and tries to stop the violence but the crowed comes out and chases the couple and the person who was saving them off stage. The two people climb down and pick up a placard with 'criminal' written and ask what it means. Yet again without a response the two people leave.

Chorus: 'আশ্রয় হবে বলে পরিবার গড়েছিল নাকি, অপরাধী সন্তান আশ্রয় হারিয়ে একাকী' *(family that was supposed to be your refuge has let you down as you are a criminal)*

House 1
House 2
Girl 1
Girl 2
Father 1
Father 2
Mother 1
Mother 2
Gender-neutral person
Public
Chorus

Scene 4

One step ladder becomes the stretcher in which a gay man is brought to the doctor by his family. The doctor examines him while the father, mother and sister wait and cry. The doctor decides to give him electroconvulsive (shock) therapy and prepares with the help of two male nurses. The other step ladder becomes the mental hospital, the family leaves him incarcerated inside the mental hospital, even though he begs them not to. He picks up the poster with 'Mental hospital' written on it and asks the audience silently whether he deserves to be treated this way.

Chorus: 'কাকে বলে রোগী, কেই বা সুস্থ, হিসাব মেলেনা আর, ভালবাসা পায় রোগের তকমা, সমাজ যে ডাক্তার' *(who is diseased and who is not, it's hard to tell you now love today is the disease as society is playing the doctor)*

Nurse 1
Nurse 2
Doctor
Gay man
Father
Mother
Sister

Scene 5

One ladder remains at the centre stage. IPC 377 (Indian Penal Code no. 377, a draconian law created by the British in 1870 effective till date that criminalizes homosexual act in India) enters and takes seat right on top of the ladder. Three persons pull violently three others – a transman, a gay man and a lesbian woman to centre stage with red dupattas (body scarf) around their wrist. The three people hand over the three other to IPC 377 at which point a chanting begins 'সমকামী নারী হায় হায়, সমকামী পুরুষ নিপাত যাক, মদ্দা মেয়ে হায় হায়, মওগা, ছক্কা নিপাত যাক,' *(homo woman shame shame, homo man go to hell, butch woman shame shame, femme man go to hell) and the three centre stage performers start a puppet-like movement with IPC 377 as the puppeteer. The three persons who had brought them on stage are standing and watching the performance and clapping in enjoyment. In the middle of this performance another person (gender-neutral) enters the stage and tries to stop the puppet-show – eventually throws a rainbow-coloured dupatta at IPC377 who promptly (and confusedly) catches and the gender-neutral person yanks on it to bring IPC377 crashing down. In the commotion the three gender-neutral persons freeze along with IPC377 and the gay man, lesbian woman and transman together shout out along with the gender-neutral person who yanked down IPC 377* 'আইন ধরে মারো টান, তিনশোসাতাত্তর থান থান' *(drag down the law itself and 377 will fall down) and in the second cry the people from the background join in to sing the last slogan of the play* 'ভয় দেখালেও ভয় পাবোনা জেনে রেখো; আমার ভাষা, আমার ভাষ্য মনে রেখো' *(you can dare but I won't fear as it's my life that I desire you can dare but I won't fear as it's my script I scripted here)*

Lesbian

Gay

Trans

IPC 377

Gender-neutral person who pulls down 377

Person 1 (puller)
Person 2 (puller)
Person 3 (puller)
Public

The street theatre workshops were devised and conducted through the multiple experiences of the eleven people who joined the research team with Niharika, Sumita and Rukmini. The three-day preparatory workshops culminated into performances on the fourth day at Ranuchhaya Arena and Y Channel, Esplanade. The Ranuchhaya Arena holds the Academy of Fine Arts and Rabindrasadan auditoriums. It is a popular social/art space for the city's middle to upper class. The place is also frequented by young adults and students looking to catch a programme/play/art exhibition, protest and meet. The Y Channel, Esplanade is a busy spot in one of the hearts of the city's business and commuting locales. It holds several small businesses and vendors and is witness to daily migrants who come to the city from the suburbs looking for work.

The workshops were facilitated by Sumita; they began with warm-up exercises, concentrating on body movements that acted also as an icebreaker. Following that, the participants were divided into two groups for the rest of the day's activities. Each group was asked to create one commercial and one item number. Both the groups decided to present a commercial in the form of an item number. The same two groups were asked to coordinate and create a silent tableau in five scenes (a scene depicting an event of importance, by a group of performers) using their bodies as tools. One group showed the immense violence that queer, lesbian and transmasculine couples face regularly. With each tableau, the representation of the intensity of violence increased, culminating in a couple-suicide. The other began with violence, but the last two scenes showed the couple recovering and turning towards creating resistance. There were debates on the acting processes and forms of expressions that the group would take up for the performance, and we decided to make it a cross between poster play, body theatre and voiceover drama by holding up Bangla placards as dialogues, using voiceovers as emotion boosters, with background music fillers and exaggerated, suggestive body language. The locations were also decided after heated conversations about public spaces in Kolkata. The two places that were finalized offered two different sets of audiences for the performances, one a lower-to-lower-middle-class working space, with a lot of transiting foot falls, mostly not the theatre going, 'arty' type crowd, the other being a marked space for art, music and theatre in particular, where people expect performances of resistance as common occurrence.

Through the process of the day-long workshops, the participants exchanged stories, decided on characters and took ownership of the script and the performance. The performers were given handouts with short one-lined themes that they used to develop some of the sequences. These themes were an initial set of 'findings' from the project workshops. Primarily the script took shape around the themes of violence and discrimination (that makes life unliveable) and community activism (that makes life liveable). We also decided to create leaflets to distribute to the audience, which could contain some information and awareness about the realities of LGBTQ identifying persons and Sappho for Equality's contact information.

The second and the third days of the workshop series went to rehearsing and modifying some of the scenes. A significant event on the second day was deciding the scene arrangement and micro-tweaking. By this time, the team had critical feedback from the participants and some members of Sappho for Equality who were with the team as observers and helping with the arrangements. One of the significant issues was that the team had to incorporate different forms of violence and discrimination, both overt and covert. Over the years, the nature of violence and discrimination has changed, and therefore the team wanted to show the variations in the performance. Thus, in keeping with this, one of the scenes that were supposed to happen in an outdoor setup (a street) was changed to a scene in front of a public toilet. During another critical discussion, another issue from the group was the medical fraternity's treatment of lesbian identifying and transmasculine persons. A new scene was born, inspired by a real-life story of a young cis-male person and his struggle with his family's extreme violence after trying to 'come out' to his parents. Another important discussion was about the possibility of using live music to gather a crowd right before the performance started, as is the way of many Indian rural performing genres, like *Yatra* (typical of West Bengal and other Bangla-speaking regions), *Nautanki* (typical of Bihar, Uttar Pradesh and some other Hindi speaking regions), *Yakshagana* (typical of Karnataka and some of the other southern Indian states), etc. But the team had to settle with a recorded version of the song written by Sumita, inspired by *gambeera* music, as creating live music was beyond their scope of performances. Since the mutual decision was to keep speech to a minimum, the participants had to master body movements and synchronize all collective actions with the help of some symbolic objects like *bindi*, step-ladder, *gamchha*, branches of trees, moustache, etc., to express various characters, places, emotions and events.

The performance opened with a scene at a public park where same-gender lovers were abused; following this was the public toilet scene where a transman was refused entry to the 'female' marked restroom. The next scene showed familial violence when two cis-women were forced apart by their respective sets of parents with physical and emotional violence; the second last scene was that of a same gender-loving person's trials and tribulations at a mental hospital. The ending was a culmination of all these repeated scenes (and spaces) of violence coming to an end when a person with no gender-sexuality markers came out to literally 'topple down' Section 377. Repeated chanting of the slogan 'ভয় দেখালেও ভয় পাবোনা জেনে রেখো, আমার ভাষা আমার ভাষ্য মনে রেখো' (threaten me as you want, but remember: I will script my script) brought the play to a thundering end.

Overall, the script spoke of violence, discrimination, resistance and community bonding. It reflected some of the stories that emerged from the project workshops from lesbian identifying and transmasculine individuals who were living covert lives in the urban peripheries of Kolkata for their 'inability' to align with the 'mainstream'.[10] The song, the slogans and the placards created to communicate with the audience were entirely the outcome of inventive thinking and deep reflections by the team members around questions of violence at different institutional sites and public spaces from family members, and strangers, medical professionals and government agencies. Most participants embodied memories of varying physical and emotional violations from these sites and carried narratives that found their way into the script. The crafters of the script were also aware of the im/possibilities of performing under a regime that was increasing its surveillance and consequent fear of losing their jobs. Hence a decision was taken to paint the face white and accentuate the eyes to hold on to anonymity while enhancing the theatrical value of the performance as the mime performers. The group was excited to present 'I script my script' to people who were strangers and came from diverse socio-economic-political backgrounds.

The first performance was done at Y-Channel, Esplanade. There was a small market and a large bus terminus right next to us, so we attracted vendors, merchants, travellers, passer-byes, friends who were invited and some uncategorized strangers. People in this area are usually not used to watching street performances, as they are way more conversant with political gatherings which often turn nasty. So, they were, in the beginning, somewhat sceptical of the performing team. The music worked well in this space, the catchy tune and interesting lyric interspersed with words like সমকামী/*samakamee* (desiring the same), হিজড়া/*hijra*, কতি/*koti*, usually not used freely in everyday conversations, attracted people.

And once the performance started, audience started to gather, and finally an interesting scene enacted itself outside the performance area, where some of the audience along with some police personnel started moving rhythmically with আমার ভাষা আমার ভাষ্য / *Amar Bhasha Amar Bhashya (I will script my script)* chant. That was a beautiful moment of spatial transaction between the supposed 'us and them'. The second performance was at the Ranuchhaya Arena, which brought a different set of audience that included students, artists, movie-lovers and heterosexual couples looking to spend some time together on a Sunday evening. There was already a small crowd, and when we started to blare the catchy song, people began to gather around the small dais. The second performance started smoothly as the performers were much more relaxed, but their energies and connections were more robust. By the end of the play, there was a big crowd. The audience interaction highlighted some important concepts carried by 'non-LGBTQ' persons, some of whom were empathetic while others were questioning, and still, others were offensive. It was pertinent also because the US Supreme Court legalized 'gay marriage' the previous day, so some people in the Ranuchhaya arena were particularly aware of the ongoing global discussions around LGBTQ politics, connecting the transnational scenes. At the end of both the performances, the team briefly interviewed some of the audience members to receive feedback on the play and assess the impact. Even though the performers were silent, through music, posters, placards, leaflets and voiceover, the performances could communicate with the audience; it allowed for a portrayal of a certain kind of dissent, created in common yet also through a disconnect of extra/ordinary.

As some participants and facilitators highlighted, the theatre workshop and performance across June 2015 were part of our 'collective liveability'. The realities that many participants occupied as young queer and trans-individuals were at times isolating and filled with an intense need to connect with other movements. By the time the play was being performed, we were contending with various dominant representations of queer and trans-persons lives while trying to (re)politicize the self with one's own life and the intimate and non-intimate others, renewal of relationships and sharing stories. For Sappho for Equality, this was an advocacy tool to engage people on the streets around what not/liveable means.

The theatre workshops and final performances happened through June of 2015, which were an intense one month of collective introspection, observation and finally finding ways to perform of our un/liveabilities. Participants of the Kolkata theatre workshops consisted of queer, lesbian and trans identifying individuals with gender assigned female at birth. They were on the one hand trying to legitimize their ordinary experiences of violence and resistance and, on the other, attempting to create their own stories against the dominant narratives of queer and trans-lives played out by the mainstream. The act of commoning in particular space-time of this series of theatre workshops and the culminating performances for them became, in their own words, a space and time of 'collective liveabilities'. A (re)politicization the self in relation to intimate and non-intimate others, and renewal of relationships and sharing stories happened in this endeavour to create a fleeting commons in the space of the month. This for Sappho for Equality was a beautiful and meaningful expression as the collective-based organization was and still is looking for such moments, expressions and ideas to be used as advocacy material.

Performing liveabilities in Brighton

Brighton Theatre Workshop Session Plan
Please ask the participants to eat a hearty breakfast as we will break for lunch at 14.00.
11.00 to 12.00
Self-introduction (we need to know their special interest and abilities that can be used for the play)
Participants will be put into pairs and one will introduce the other through a charade. Participants will be asked to create an advertisement copy about them selling themselves as products.
Participants will create a situation involving at least one imaginary person to introduce themselves.
Participants will introduce themselves as a non-human entity or thing and explain why.

Group building exercise/trust games
Participants will stand in a tight circle and one person will stand in the middle with eyes closed. S/he will fall in any direction and will trust her/his friends/partners to break the fall. Each participant will be given three unrelated words (tree, train, toad or rain, rice, rattle or dog, door, disc) by which they will create a situation in not more than three sentences. Then the group will come together and weave a meaningful story using these sentences together. Participants will be divided into three groups and the facilitator will call out the name of an emotion. The group will have to create a situation (using body and facial expressions) that depicts that emotion.
12.00 to 12.15
Short tea/coffee/smoke break

12.15 to 14.00
Participants will be divided into three groups. Each group will be assigned to discuss LGBTQ lives as they experience personally and from people they know. Whether these lives are liveable

and/or unliveable and why. They will present their discussion in the large group.

In the second phase, the participants will be regrouped and will be asked to change the unliveablities into liveabiliities if possible, using factors that contribute to liveabilities.

By the end of the exercise we will have a list of factors that contribute to liveabilities, some to unliveabilities and some ways to change an unliveable situation towards a liveable one.

14.00 to 14.45

Lunch

14.45 to 18.00 (including a fifteen-minute tea/coffee/smoke break)

Participants will be divided into three groups, if possible, according to their special abilities. Each group will be asked to create a scene focusing upon the findings of the group exercise before lunch. They can create posters, write a script using dialogues or may use mime. They can use other props and materials that we already have. They can create a song-dance number, a silent tableau (series of static figures depicting a scene) or any other form they chose and a combination of everything. The facilitators will help the groups connect with each other at the end to have a three-scene play of about ten to twelve minutes. We may give it a name, or may call it 'I Script My script' as the Kolkata participants wanted.

AND WE GO OUT TO PLAY!

In the summer of 2015, Sumita, Debalina and Niharika travelled to Brighton to facilitate and document theatre workshops following a different methodology. For Brighton, two workshops were designed as day-long sessions ending in a performance for one weekend, a Saturday and a Sunday. This difference in methodology was based on the research team's understanding of how the queer community in two places are living their lives, whether there is a functional queer collective present in these places, what are the ideals of liveability that Brighton participants would bring forth, etc. It operationalized our transnational research methodologies in new ways.

In Kolkata, the absence of social security, legal back-up and large-scale familial acceptance has given rise to many alternative spaces and collectives, where queer and transpeople support each other emotionally as well as create different forms of resistance and movements. In Kolkata therefore the research team could work with an already-formed cohesive group, a collective who are well conversed in the language of resistance. In Brighton however, we did not work with a collective based on gender-sexual marginalization; advertisements were sent out and queer/trans-folks joined on the basis of the adverts and communication by word of mouth. So, while the research team was planning theatre workshops in Brighton, queer and trans-friends and other individuals were asked to join for a day to see how they feel about a day-long programme without any expectation. Therefore, in Brighton on the two occasions, groups of strangers and friends joined the research team to participate in the process, and the outcomes were therefore very different from Kolkata and unique in its own way.

On both the days of the workshops, the process began with group-building exercises and trust games. After the initial icebreakers, Sumita spent a reasonable amount of time to create a safe space for participants to open themselves up to the possibilities of sharing stories. From sharing stories to shared stories, the goal was to create tales of lives as experienced by individuals but expressed as a collective. To attain this end, Sumita used certain unrelated words, asked the participants to connect those to emotions and finally express those by physical gestures using the body to communicate with each other.

After this phase, participants told us that they could enter into conversations concerning not/liveable experiences related to LGBTQ identifying lives from their own, from people they know, with relative ease. Materials from the research were also used as indicators for the participants to attach their thoughts to. On the first day, four participants and three researchers queried the boundaries of identities and how they are de/attached from/ to bodies through a game of 'identity twister'. On the second day, seven participants and three researchers focused on a performance art piece that developed on words and stories participants shared in the workshop to speak to care, community and solidarities. During the performance and after, other researchers talked to the crowd, gauging reactions (overwhelmingly positive and supportive) and speaking to them about the purpose of the performance/the *Liveable Lives* project.

The performances happened at a local public park on Saturday and Brighton sea-front on Sunday. The Saturday performance in the park was not well attended, with people spread all over the park, and they did not move closer even when invited. Brighton is often understood as 'accepting', 'diverse', 'equal', rendering LGBTQ lives 'normal'. Whilst evidence shows (Browne & Bakshi, 2013) and our participants told us that this is not the case, the tepid response reflects the presumption of LGBTQ lives as already 'sorted' in a city that has branded itself as 'the gay capital'.[11] Seeking to contest public space that is understood as 'accepting' was a key pivot for the workshops and the performances, which could be seen as 'failing' to engage onlookers in the way that the Kolkata workshops did. Such considerations are represented in the documentary film,[12] illustrating the limitations of experimental methods that can be written in overly celebratory ways. Nonetheless, there were positives and potentials in the Brighton workshops for those who participated.

Debalina, our filmmaker, had interviewed all the participants, bringing out crosscutting issues of race, ethnic identities, language, mental health and much more, along with gender-sexual orientations. It clearly came out that Brighton may not marginalize queer/trans-people, but can have issues with other identities, juxtaposed with queer/trans. The question of overlapping and intersectional identities, and how it affects one's liveability was the central theme for day 1's performance and the participants very aptly reflected on the lack of interest from the general population present in the public park. If liveability is about only getting one's rights, then the queer and trans-community in Brighton has it all, and participants felt that people are not interested in knowing what goes beyond that, who falls through the gaps in the game of identity twister. Consider this excerpt from Debalina's interviews with the participants after the performances got over:

> The reason why I joined the workshop today, I was interested in the element of street theatre to get involved in something which would be an intervention of public space in Brighton as liberal city. People even dubbed Brighton as San Francisco of Britain. Yet, it is important to explain LGBTQ public space, how boundaries of the city are constructed through social identification of places in the city. So, for me today to join a group of people whom I didn't know, something so important when you collaborate, when you do something, you don't know. So, you build up, do something. I desired to make an intervention in the public space in Brighton and also to do something with the people I didn't know.

The Brighton street theatre experience had brought together a commoning amongst the participants rather than the audience. Strangers and friends coming together for a day to create something which is owned by all, a script written by all, curated out of something that talks about the dreams, wishes and heartbreaks of individuals, created a different kind of bonding, of queer/trans-people coming together over exploring their liveabilities and questioning their lives in the process. Since the *Liveable Lives* research team had no idea of what to expect, everything that came out through the process was unique. Participants bonded, shared, talked about their personal experiences of un/liveability, and created a shared vision even if for a short span of time. As Kath said:

> I had the idea of a flash mob and discussed it with Niharika, and she was quite excited. She told me about using street theatre as a political idea act that could change or get to the point where we understood something get to change space for a short period of time, to be able to have time and space as we want. So as a part of the project, we didn't just want to understand something; we also wanted to have a go at change, even if it is for a few seconds or minutes, maybe people in the workshop, people seeing the workshop, or people watching this video will want to bring in some change in those few moments which will add up and maybe that would make life become liveable for LGBT people across UK and India.

The performance on the second day by the Brighton seaside had some casual viewers, but many walked past not keen enough to acknowledge the uniqueness of the presentation taking place on that sunny afternoon. The theme for Sunday was how to creatively bring together the individual ideas of liveability in one space, where each individual can contribute, yet remain unique. It seemed a difficult theme, but the participants became so much invested in each other's ideas that it became a beautiful rhythm, a creative collaborative performance, almost like a dance. One of the participants commented after:

> It was the quite safe space, so I could express myself freely; there was no fear. I could say what I want to say. It was nice to be able to share. Hear other people's opinions about the subject of the queer. I like the creativity. So, I like the elements there. While we were trying to work something, intersect the stories, it was interesting. The process of it was interesting, and it was just interesting to see people from different backgrounds. So that was interesting, to share a kind of experience. It was nice to see different experience of the LGBT people.

This whole experience of participating in a process, with back-to-back workshops and performances, brought out different emotions and meanings for different participants. But what remained important for the research team was the idea of a collective taking shape through it. It was momentary, it was fleeting, perhaps it was the excitement of being part of something for the first time for some of the participants had made their experience so positive. Whatever it was, even for a fleeting moment the collective and the commons emerged out of those individuals. Even if they do not/cannot carry it forward, it was clear that they enjoyed it, learned, connected and believed in new worlds:

> We got on very well today. I met somebody, [the] relationship will continue beyond today. It's [theatre] led to the creation of relationships that will survive a long way.
>
> I'm new to Brighton, it's been eighteen months, and this will be one of those things that I look back on which will remind me of why I got rooted in Brighton. This brought me together, with creative thinking queer people. And if you ask me what makes life liveable, it is other creative, queer, thinking people.

Conclusion

Street theatre has significant potential as performances that experiment in creating social change momentarily within and beyond the discourse of equalities and rights. Considering the possibilities of commonplace, street theatre both enables the creation of practices in common and can act as an extraordinary moment. Where LGBTQ identifying lives are seen as normal, the disruption promised by street theatre can be more easily ignored and overlooked. In Brighton we found that the disruption was less important than the commonalities created between those who attend workshops. The performative aspects of liveability and their temporal possibilities in place can be deployed to place sexual and gender politics in the here inhabited by street theatre participants and performers and offer a potential of something else, something more liveable, even with their limitations.

Placing street theatre is vital. It matters where they occur. Whilst elsewhere in the book, our work has addressed more broadly England/West Bengal, the street theatres were in, and of, Kolkata and Brighton. They drew on and reiterated the places where they occurred and reworked, reimagined and momentarily recreated them. In Kolkata, the contestation of normative streets drew attention as participants in song and face paints asked 'not to disregard anyone'. In Brighton, the 'gay city' loomed in participants' narratives, motivations for creating the workshops and the reception of the street theatre performances.

This does not deny the import of connections, networks, solidarities and commonalities. Kolkata and Brighton, while spatially very different, embodied a collective effort and spirit through the physical movements, the tactile sensations, the words, songs and feelings of safety. There were connections of multiple forms, only some of which can be named and many of which transcended the project itself through friendships and connections, including in the creation of this book. Yet, there remained imaginings of place that saw Kolkata as impoverished, less than Brighton, an 'other place' that can be exoticised but remains dangerous.

Ultimately, as participants in the workshops and performances shared, performing liveability became an act of liveability itself. The possibility of change, while always in becoming, was held together by affective moments and physical actions with/in one's limits of the body, mind and life situations. Through the processes of group exercises, character building and script creation, our workshops and theatres across Kolkata and Brighton brought together several scenes of power and life-affirming incidents. Each was spatially and temporally specific but also held together with stories from other lives and places. Performing liveabilities through street theatre offered an embodied gesture to create (fleeting?) liveabilities for selves and others.

Afterword

We complete this book with thoughts from our collaborators. We asked Leela and Sumita three questions, which they spoke to. They pointed us towards the afterlife of *Liveable Lives* to considerations of new horizons. Connecting this to a thread from our acknowledgements, we hope that liveability will find more lives, objects and issues to deepen our critical empirical understanding of sexual and gendered politics. We see these journeys as unfinished, even for ourselves, and this afterward reflects this.

We begin with Leela's relies to our email prompts.

What do you remember of Liveable Lives?

I remember the gatherings of people. Meetings, meeting our colleagues from India arriving at Brighton station, a zoom meeting with the UK collective, people coming to our data collection/exploring the question event at friends meeting house, people gathering, and taking it in as they walked past, at the street theatre on the seafront…

I think these may be such big stand-out moments in the context of not meeting, not connecting through pandemic restrictions.

What are the things that stick with you?

What sticks with me is friendly goodwill and sharing. A feeling of freedom to wander. Connection and sharing.

What would you want others to know and do/not do?

I am imagining talking with others in community activism. I would want to share about the international, that academics call transnational, aspect of the project. That we looked at the same question in different places but the method for exploring and specific questions don't have to be the same. I remember Nick doing interviews with one-off connections in Hull and more of a drop in collective interactive mingling in Brighton and interviews in the context of connections through community and friendships in Kolkata, and less familiar elsewhere in West Bengal. That working with different perspectives, with very unfamiliar situations alongside stories related from a more familiar context, gives a different connection with the data, it feels more multifaceted. That the international work can happen over zoom and email but the meeting in person, the travel undertaken feels necessary, essential to making it work. I feel political power in experiencing the connections, in reaching to work together with people in other places, towns in UK and towns in India, the (few) people joining the discussion on the liveable lives website. Different to looking at data that people pour into projects like a receptacle that they remain outside of. The India side produced the beautiful book, in Brighton there was the beautiful conference, a big question for me is how can research projects like this one provide community and support for more people who contribute. How to tackle the consumption of sharing and experience that is capital for academia and researchers, how to share that richness with a community of people who contribute?

That's my thoughts for now.

Leela

Brighton-Kolkata-Dhaka: The journey continues ...

Liveable Lives, as I understood it, was a transnational project that brought two different worlds in close proximity. But whenever I used to ponder about the LL [*Liveable Lives* project], I only thought about India, specifically Kolkata and its surrounding, where it happened for me. Brighton was a faraway place I visited twice within the tenure of the project, where I've seen happy (seeming) same-sex parents confidently pushing perambulators with sleepy babies towards their rightsfull future. Not my reality, I thought.

But as these seemingly different realities came together, at least on paper, we could clearly see that lives can become liveable with unlikely things, and those markers of liveabilities can be very queer/weird/ strange in nature. And these queer markers can quietly challenge the given structured notion of one singularly liveable life propagated by the normative world. To me this normative liveability is accentuated by the perambulators full of sleeping babies for queer Brighton, and for queer Kolkata it is a secret household of a same-sex couple, 'friend' to the rest of the world, complete with some cats. And since Brighton could openly display this singular, ideal, 'normal' liveable queer life, it has 'arrived' where it aspired to be, while the poor cousin Kolkata can only wish for such freedom and make do with whispered shadows.

This is how LL helped me see through 'arrived' Brighton and 'backward' Kolkata, to move towards singular to multiple notions of liveabilties, from straight measurement of queer lives to strange twists and turns it could offer. A perambulator can definitely be one representation of one liveable life, achieving marriage equality rights can definitely be one marker of one liveability, but they are not THE way to BE. As for me, travelling between two cities of India to create a queer living space and traversing the Himalayas, with or without my partner, is the epitome of my liveability; how do I fit myself in a list of normative markers?

This singular liveabiliy structure propagated to us is utterly lacking in providing queer space for queer people anywhere in the world.

My understanding deepened with I script My Script – the street theatre component of LL. My experience of conducting theatre workshops culminating in street plays in both Brighton and Kolkata made me question this singular notion of liveability even more. In both the places queer people participated in the process to create a temporary space where they can express their own idea of liveability and unliveability through performances. So in Brighton, steady perambulators gave way to unrest and unmet expectations, straight within the queer and vice versa colliding into each other; other factors like class, race, gender and various other identities came into play affecting individual liveability, giving rise to multiple and dynamic liveabilities. In Kolkata we saw a play growing into a momentous moment of overthrowing the normative oppressive forces that try to strangle queer lives, culminating into a song of protest. At that time around September 2015, the incriminating law IPC 377 was still effective in India, and queer Kolkata's un/liveabilities depended heavily upon that fact. I still remember those moments of connection on the streets of Brighton and Kolkata, a quest of livebilities – from singular to plural.

From liveability to liveabilities, this has been the most significant journey for me through this project, and today when I look back, I can see my already-existing belief in diversity, interconnectivity, multiplicity of thoughts, desires, notions, life experiences got a boost of critical support through LL. The LL experience helped me articulate and arrange my thoughts while working with grassroot groups to destabilize the singular notion of gender-sexual liveability and finally bring the intersectionality lens to understand life and living in a more holistic way.

Liveable Lives ended as a project in April 2016, for me and Sappho. In 2020, just before the Covid pandemic struck us down, I started working on a project of collecting first-person narratives of lesbian identifying persons from West Bengal and Bangladesh, to be published as an anthology. It was named as *Monologue – lesbian narratives from Bangladesh and West Bengal*, which got published in 2021 originally in Bangla and later translated into English. In 2019, when I started working on this project with my friend and colleague Minakshi

Sanyal Malobika at Sappho, I realized how *Liveable Lives* had stayed inside me, and how the distance of more than three years has actually helped in putting my LL experience in a better perspective for me.

Monologue was also a trans-national project, albeit of a different genre than LL. But in the South Asian context, we the Indians assume the place of Big Brother in almost everything, exactly the way Global North would assume itself in relation to Global South. For *Monologue*, therefore, Bangladesh was supposed to be the poor cousin, had we followed the route of singular liveability marker through their narratives. *Liveable Lives* project helped me comprehend the concept of trans-national work, especially when that happens between seemingly unequal partners. Between Brighton and Kolkata, Kolkata queers had no legal/social/familial support, no rights to live on their own terms and had an incriminating law to tip the scale further. On the other hand Brighton had all the necessary support systems, apart from being a part of the Global North, which made it a faraway fairyland for us. Yet Kolkata lived, sometimes barely survived, just like Brighton. Both these places dreamt their own dreams of liveabilities which brought so much colour in the spectrum.

Bangladesh still has that incriminating article 377 of Bangladesh Penal Code against same-sex loving people; it also has stringent religious rules against same-sex loving people, whereas in India IPC 377 has been read down on 6 September 2018, the Transgender Persons' Act for protecting rights of transgender people and ensuring their welfare was commenced on 10 January 2020. It made this country supposedly more 'progressive' and 'better' for queer/trans identifying people as per general belief. One part of the LGBTQI movement is indeed progressing towards the singular liveability notion, furnished with normative markers of marriage equality/civil partnership and state recognition, expecting it would bring in societal and familial recognition too. Bangladesh is so far away from this reality, or we from them, just like Brighton was from Kolkata.

Monologue reminded me of LL more often than not. I could clearly map the winding road from Brighton to Bangladesh/Dhaka via Kolkata, everywhere how interestingly the narrators talked about their lives, their triumphs, their desires and also about the utter helplessness of their existence in the same breath. Patterns of liveabilties emerged through these narratives, multitude of possibilities, each unique, yet connected and each placed in a specific geopolitical context. LL helped me look at the narratives of *Monologue* through the transnational lens; the political positioning of Brighton-Kolkata enhanced my understanding of Kolkata-Dhaka positioning, with further clarity.

For the Kolkata/West Bengal part of LL, we used to use two words to explain liveability – living and surviving. There was much interplay between these two words or notions of Being; each of our participants came up with different ways to explain themselves in terms of living and/or surviving. I personally had a notion too that living would give a better meaning to life; it would mean a life worth living and surviving would be somewhat lesser than living, just staying alive and nothing more. LL participants came up with completely different ways of looking at surviving, not as a lesser stage vis-à-vis living, but a totally independent space where a queer person can arrive after pushing out of the downstream tide of hetero/homo-normative expectations. It is a space to rest, to breathe, to ponder before jumping into life to swim upstream. Surviving is no less or more than living; it is just another space, to arrive, to be.

Monologue narrators from Dhaka/Bangladesh wanted to survive; for most of them surviving the everyday onslaught of violence at any cost was more important than anything else. They were ready to leave their country/family/friends simply to survive with their lesbian identity in any corner of the world. And the Kolkata/West Bengal narrators wanted to live larger than their single lesbian identity; they felt they must connect with other marginalized identities, collectives and movements for rights and justice, to explore their own intersectional positions as much as possible. For the Kolkata/West Bengal participants, their lesbian identity was already consolidated; they wanted to go further than that to live a larger life; for Dhaka/Bangladesh, they needed to consolidate their one identity, lesbian in this case, to survive.

LL has given me the clarity to navigate through lives, identities and desires to live, survive and make lives worth living without hierarching one over some. The journey from Brighton to Kolkata to Dhaka to some other unknown destination thus continues.

পুব থেকে পশ্চিম তুমি
আমি দক্ষিণ থেকে উত্তর
এভাবেও যোগ চিহ্ন হয়

East to West you go
North to South I traverse
Thus a plus may also appear…
(translated by Rukmini Banerjee)

Sumita

Notes

Chapter 1

1. This research was supported by the ESRC [grant number ES/M000931/1] – Making Liveable Lives: Rethinking Social Exclusion (2014–17).
2. Niharika is a member of and actively involved with Sappho for Equality (https://www.sapphokolkata.in), an organization working with lesbian women, bisexual women and transmasculine persons in eastern India.
3. Niharika's work and the collaboration with Kath to produce this book were possible through a generous visiting fellowship supported by University College Dublin.
4. We use juridico-political as a shorthand for institutional relations of power that cross law/courts/justice systems/governments. This includes equalities legislations, court decisions, etc., that form a key basis for discussion. However, we are not specifically engaging with this concept or seeking to detail rational/rationalizing power that runs over legal and political institutional landscape. Instead, our focus is on understanding what makes life liveable for LGBTQ identifying people, and how this can be desired, an ideal that might only ever be partially and momentarily achieved.
5. We would query the potential binary between liveable/unliveable and the spatial/temporal conditionalities of liveability that means life can be both liveable/not liveable simultaneously. See Chapter 4 where we discuss how life may be both simultaneously. Thus, we speak about what makes life (not) liveable.
6. The purpose of this book is not to explore the literature in rethinking liveabilities through historical social movements and liberation politics within and before legal recognition. Such work of course could be valuable in naming and exploring the longevity of seeking a life that is a life for LGBTQ identifying people.

7   The Kiss of Love protests began in Kerala in November 2014 and then ran through several iterations in a few Indian cities until February 2015. For more on the protest and its connection to Hindu right-wing moral policing, see J. Devika (2021).
8   The Bangla transliterations are part of everyday speech acts, but their usefulness in connecting to the English term 'liveability' was discussed.
9   During the course of this research, Niharika changed institutions from the University of Southern Indiana to Ambedkar University, Delhi.
10 Video can be found here: https://www.youtube.com/watch?v=PG1OQbimNvk or for a shorter version see here: https://www.youtube.com/watch?v=DnHHu-v84ko, for the Kolkata workshop see here: https://www.youtube.com/watch?v=QfKZSnJzgj8&list=PLfEABXevqzjjfgAClaLWXs_RyQFDyN8Wl
11 On 6 September 2018, the Supreme Court of India, in the Navtej Singh Johar vs. Union of India case, read down Section 377 of the Indian Penal Code, the anti-sodomy colonial law, in effect recognizing consensual sexual acts other than peno-vaginal ones. The project work was completed prior to the 6 September verdict.
12 This narrative is of course easily problematized, for example, the National Legal Services Authority (NALSA) vs. Union of India verdict gave trans-people in India the ability to seek welfare on 5 April 2014; yet, this verdict was explicitly worded so as not to interfere with the recent re-criminalization of IPC 377 (Sheikh 2014 – http://orinam.net/content/wp-content/uploads/2014/04/nalsa_summary_danish.pdf).
13 As can be seen in table, there are specific geographies within Great Britain as to where data was collected. These vary across England/Great Britain/UK. Similarly, the research was predominantly undertaken in West Bengal. We use specific regions/nations where these can be named and UK/India where these are implicated, for example, in questionnaire data. The project does not seek to be representative and more geographical nuances are always required and welcomed.
14 The project and the book do not delve into a history of the circulation of LGBTQ in postcolonial contexts. For a recent historical look, see Katyal (2016) and Khanna (2016).

Chapter 2

1. In this chapter, we work with the assumption that the geographies of southern and northern contexts may not fall squarely onto national maps.
2. The locus of Eurocentric thought, while emerging from the histories of Enlightenment in Anglo-American worlds, need not necessarily be tied to the Global North; rather the geographies of Eurocentrism may be in 'non-European' worlds as well, in their imbrication with contextual power relations such as that of Brahmanical orders.
3. For the difference between dwelling and residence, see Mignolo (2011a, location 441). Kindle edition.
4. Scheduled Caste is an official term to refer to broad categories of social groups marginalized by caste, who are the targets of administrative and welfare reforms.
5. Navtej Singh Johar and Others vs. Union of India.
6. A Bench comprising then Chief Justice A. P. Shah and Justice S. Murlidhar in its 105-page judgement had said that criminalization of homosexuality among consenting adults is a violation of Article 14 (guarantees equality before the law), Article 15 (prohibits discrimination on grounds of religion, race, caste, sex or place of birth) and Article 21 (guarantees protection of life and personal liberty) of the Constitution of India. They said, 'As it stands, Section 377 denies a gay person a right to full personhood which is implicit in notion of life under Article 21 of the Constitution.'
7. A two-judge bench, comprising Justice G. S. Singhvi and Justice S. J. Mukhopadhaya observed that the HC had overlooked the fact that a 'miniscule fraction of the country's population constitute LGBT', and that in over 150 years less than 200 people were prosecuted for committing offence under the section. https://indianexpress.com/article/india/section-377-to-be-revisited-timeline-of-the-case-5016095/
8. In Great Britain, in addition to the Marriage (Same-Sex Couples) Act 2013, more than a decade of piecemeal legislation around sexuality and gender identity was unified under the Equality Act 2010. This Act

upholds wide-ranging protections against discrimination for LGBTQ people under the Protected Characteristics of 'Sexual Identity' and 'Gender Reassignment'. The latter of which, at the time of writing in late 2021, is under contestation from 'Gender Critical' women and others.

9   Five-judge Constitutional bench, led by Chief Justice of India Dipak Misra and comprising Justices R. F. Nariman, A. M. Khanwilkar, D. Y. Chandrachud and Indu Malhotra, stated Section 377 to be unconstitutional.

10 Mignolo (2011a) elaborates body-politics of knowledge or bio-graphics to connote the 'responses, thinking and action, of the population who do not want to be managed by the state and want to delink from the technologies of power to which they are being summated' (Mignolo, 2011a, location 625). Opposed to body-politics is bio-politics or biopower that connotes strategies of the state to govern populations.

11 Mignolo (2011a) reminds that the 'translation of geography into chronology was the work of colonization' and 'has served as the justification of the ideology of progress and, in the twentieth century of development and underdevelopment' (151).

12 Mignolo (2011a) notes that this term was introduced by Adolfo Alban Achinte to talk about how Afro-Colombian communities in Columbia from the eighteenth to twentieth centuries create forms of re-existences rather than resistances.

13 Epistemic disobedience means changing the terms of the conversation underlining the colonial matrix of power. For more on this, see Mignolo (2011a).

14 For more on how we theorize transnational feminist queer methodologies, see Browne, Kath, Niharika Banerjea, Nick McGlynn, Sumita B., Leela Bakshi, Rukmini Banerjee and Ranjita Biswas. 2017. 'Towards Transnational Feminist Queer Methodologies.' *Gender, Place and Culture*. DOI: 10.1080/0966369X.2017.1372374

15 Rukmini Banerjee was recruited as a Research Associate through a rigorous interview process.

16 We offered participants' different forms of maps that included an outline of countries. We ask ourselves, if providing such outlines reproduces dualisms? In one sense, yes, but on the other, our purpose was to use the maps in circulation to understand if that would provoke different readings of the same.

17 The participant is referring to *Ebong Bewarish* (… and the unclaimed), 2013, a film by Debalina and produced by Sappho for Equality.

Chapter 3

1 See GEO (2010).

2 This was undertaken by reviewing local government websites to check fulfilment of a core duty of the Equality Act, which required publication of information to show compliance with the Act, and as a source of information about implementation of other duties of the Equality Act 2010. The premise was that information about equalities work would be made 'publicly accessible' through publication on local authority websites. Where information could not be found on websites, data collection was supplemented by requesting information directly from the local government organization. A desk-based search of information published on websites for the 353 local authorities in England, which are charged with the implementation of legislation at a local level, was carried out between November 2014 and January 2015 (see Browne et al., 2016).

The legislative demands are most clearly spelled out in the Act itself and in a set of guidelines produced by the Government Equalities Office (GEO, 2010).

3 See also Matthews (2020).

4 Khap panchayats are caste-based territorial social groups in northwest India that exercise social control in their villages, especially with reference to love and marriage. For a socio-historical view of khap panchayats, see Kumar (2012). Post the Naz Judgement, several khaps had sought a triple ban on 'homosexuality, embryo transplant and surrogate motherhood' (Deswal, 2010).

5   See Sharma and Kaul (2009). Also, note that at the time of this phase of the work, 2014/15, the UK also banned gay men from donating blood if they have had penetrative sex within the past year.
6   Ruth Vanita and Saleem Kidwai (2000) have created an academic archive on homoerotic affinities in ancient and medieval India. Their archival research has brought attention to homoerotic embodiment in several representational sites, including paintings, temple carvings, epics and poetry. The eleventh-century group of Khajuraho temples and thirteenth-century Konark temple carry carvings of humans in erotic-intimate positions.
7   Ruth Vanita has historically traced the way marriage has been perceived over the years in Vedic Hindu traditions. A notable point in her work (2005) that often gets referred to is the Hindu Marriage Act, 1955, which specifies the coming together of spirits without any mention of 'sex' or 'gender'.
8   Marriage for same gender couples is not legalized in India. Yet, same-gender couples often get married in either temples (if a priest is willing to officiate the ceremonies) or perform Hindu rituals to socially sanction their unions. For more on marriage between same-gender couples, see Vanita (2005).
9   The liberatory aspect of marriage for same-gender persons, especially of two cis-women from economically modest middle-class households, and transmasculine persons lies in its potential to escape violence from family.
10 'Jawan' is the Hindi term for soldier.
11 The BJP is the ruling political party since 2014, and right-wing Hindu fundamentalist.
12 The Congress party (Indian National Congress) was the ruling government during the time of the media analysis. The BJP was in the opposition along with the CPI(M) (Communist Party of India (Marxist)).
13 In project workshops in India, participants' names were not recorded to preserve anonymity.

14 Equality Impact Assessments are used in England (and elsewhere) to assess the impact of particular measures and policies on marginalized groups identified in the Equalities Act 2010.
15 L.B. reads as lesbian. It is a colloquial term used amongst younger LGBTQ people from the suburbs.

Chapter 4

1 Heterosexual matrix is 'that grid of cultural intelligibility through which bodies, gender and desires are naturalized … a hegemonic discursive/epistemic model of gender intelligibility that assumes that for bodies to cohere and make sense there must be a stable sex expressed through a stable gender … that is oppositionally and hierarchically defined through compulsory practice of heterosexuality' (Butler, 1990: 208).
2 For a colonial and imperial history of the heterosexual matrix, see Patil (2018).
3 A temple. This points to the commonplace occurrences of non-normative marriages in temples in India.

Chapter 5

1 The idea and work of key individuals such as Safdar Hashmi, Badal Sarkar, Prabir Guha and questions around the theatre of the oppressed informed the making of the workshops and theatre performances, led by Sumita.
2 Sumita designed the performance and workshop scripts.
3 All the videos can be accessed here: https://www.youtube.com/user/LiveableLives
4 Item numbers are Bollywood songs infused with affect, eros and desirous displays in excess of everyday living.

5   This film is available for viewing here (https://www.youtube.com/watch?v=QfKZSnJzgj8)
6   See https://www.youtube.com/watch?v=QfKZSnJzgj8 for a visual representation of Kolkata street theatre.
7   This script is translated from Bangla.
8   Electroshock therapy machine.
9   A music-based theatrical performance genre from the north-central districts of West Bengal.
10 The 'mainstream', as an English word, was often used by our participants to suggest the unmarked socially dominant heterosexual identifying individuals, including those having privileges of class-caste and mastery over English language.
11 It might also reflect the ways in which street theatre and performance art can be commonplace on Brighton's streets/seafront/parks.
12 The film can be viewed here: https://www.youtube.com/watch?v=PG1OQbimNvk

References

Adebayo, B. & I. Kottasova, (2018), 'Denmark withholds nearly $10 million in aid money to Tanzania', *CNN*, 15 November. Available at: https://edition.cnn.com/2018/10/31/africa/tanzania-anti-gay-mass-arrests-intl/index.html (accessed 30 May 2022).

Ahmed, S., (2007), 'Multiculturalism and the promise of happiness', *New Formations*, 63(1), 121–37.

Ahmed, S., (2010), *The Promise of Happiness*, Duke University Press.

Ahmed, S., (2014), 'Imposition', *Feministkilljoys*, 14 April. Available at: http://feministkilljoys.com/2014/04/14/imposition/ (accessed 30 May 2022).

Alexander, M. J. & C. T. Mohanty, (1997), *Feminist Genealogies, Colonial Legacies, Democratic Futures*, Routledge.

Ambedkar, B. R., (1936), *Annihilation of Caste*, Verso Books.

Bacchetta, P., (2013), 'Queer formations in (Hindu) nationalism', in S. Srivastava (ed.), *Sexuality Studies*, Oxford University Press, 121–39.

Bacchetta, P. & J. Haritaworn, (2016), 'There are many transatlantics: Homonationalism, homotransnationalism and feminist–queer–trans of colour theories and practices', in K. Davis & M. Evans (eds.), *Transatlantic Conversations*, Routledge, 127–44.

Badgett, M. V., (2014), 'The economic cost of stigma and the exclusion of LGBT people: A case study of India', *World Bank Group*, 3 October. Available at: https://openknowledge.worldbank.org/handle/10986/21515 (accessed 30 May 2022).

Bakshi, S., S. Jivraj & S. Posocco, (2016), 'Introduction', in S. Bakshi, S. Jivraj & S. Posocco (eds.), *Decolonizing Sexualities: Transnational Perspectives, Critical Interventions*, Counterpress, 1–17.

Banerjea, N. & K. Browne, (2018), 'A transnational queer-feminist reflection on sexuality, development and governance', in C. L. Mason (ed.), *Routledge Handbook of Queer Development Studies*, Routledge, 169–80.

Banerjea, N., D. Dasgupta, R. Dasgupta & J. M. Grant, (2018), 'Introduction', in N. Banerjea, D. Dasgupta, R. Dasgupta & J. M. Grant (eds.), *Friendship as Social Justice Activism: Critical Solidarities in a Global Perspective*, Seagull, 1–8.

Banerjea, N., K. Browne, L. Bakshi & S. Ghosh, (2016), 'Writing through activisms and academia: Challenges and possibilities', in G. Brown & K. Browne (eds.), *The Routledge Research Companion to Geographies of Sex and Sexualities*, Routledge, 199–208.

Banerjea, N., K. Browne, E. Ferreira, M. Olasik & J. Podmore, (2019), *Lesbian Feminism: Essays Opposing Global Heteropatriarchies*, Bloomsbury Publishing.

Batchelor, T., (2017), 'One of the world's most homophobic countries is about to have a transgender model appear at fashion week', *The Independent*, 9 January. Available at: http://www.independent.co.uk/news/world/asia/india-transgender-model-anjali-lama-homophobia-lakma-fashion-weekstyle-lgbt-rights-nepalese-trans-a7517481.html (accessed 9 May 2022).

Bell, D. & J. Binnie, (2000), *The Sexual Citizen: Queer Politics and Beyond*, Polity.

Bell, D. & G. Valentine (eds.), (1995), *Mapping Desire: Geographies of Sexuality*, Routledge.

Bell, V., (2008), 'From performativity to ecology: On Judith Butler and matters of survival', *Subjectivity*, 25(1), 395–412.

Binnie, J., (2004), *The Globalization of Sexuality*, Sage.

Biswas, R., N. Banerjea, R. Banerjee & B. Sumita, (2016), 'Understanding liveability/ies: A report of "Making liveable lives: Rethinking social exclusion", A transnational activist-academic research project by Sappho for equality, India and University of Brighton, UK', *Sappho for Equality*, 26 March. Available at: http://www.sapphokolkata.in/wp-content/uploads/2016/07/SAPPHO-Liveability-Book.pdf (accessed 30 May 2022).

Biswas, R., S. Beethi & S. Ghosh, (2019), 'Manoeuvring feminisms through LGBTQ movements in India', in K. Browne, N. Banerjea, E. Ferreira, M. Olasik & J. Podmore (eds.), *Lesbian Feminism: Essays Opposing Global Heteropatriarchies*, Zed Books, 103–14.

Boyce, P. & A. Dutta, (2013), 'Vulnerability of gay and transgender Indians goes way beyond Section 377', *The Conversation*, 15 December. Available at: https://theconversation.com/vulnerability-of-gay-and-transgender-indians-goes-way-beyond-section-377-21392 (accessed 30 May 2022).

Boyce, P. & R. K. Dasgupta, (2018), 'Alternating sexualities', in S. Srivastava, Y. Arif & J. Abraham (eds.), *Critical Themes in Indian Sociology*, SAGE Publications, 330–45.

Brown, G., (2009), 'Thinking beyond homonormativity: Performative explorations of diverse gay economies', *Environment and Planning A*, 41(6), 1496–510.

Brown, G., (2012), 'Homonormativity: A metropolitan concept that denigrates "ordinary" gay lives', *Journal of Homosexuality*, 59(7), 1065–72.

Brown, G. & K. Browne, (2016), *The Routledge Research Companion to Geographies of Sex and Sexualities*, Routledge.

Brown, G. & D. Borisa, (2021), 'Making space for queer desire in global urbanism', in M. Lancione & C. McFarlane (eds.), *Global Urbanism: Knowledge, Power and the City*, Routledge, 49–55.

Browne, K., (2004), 'Genderism and the bathroom problem: (Re) materialising sexed sites, (re) creating sexed bodies', *Gender, Place & Culture*, 11(3), 331–46.

Browne, K., (2006), '"A right geezer-bird (man-woman)": The sites and sights of "Female"Embodiment', *ACME: An International Journal for Critical Geographies*, 5(2), 121–43.

Browne, K., (2007a), '(Re) making the other, heterosexualising everyday space', *Environment and Planning A*, 39(4), 996–1014.

Browne, K., (2007b), 'A party with politics? (Re) making LGBTQ Pride spaces in Dublin and Brighton', *Social & Cultural Geography*, 8(1), 63–87.

Browne, K. & L. Bakshi, (2013), *Ordinary in Brighton?: LGBT, Activisms and the City*, Routledge.

Browne, K. & C. J. Nash, (2010), *Queer Methods and Methodologies: Intersecting Queer Theories and Social Science Research*, Taylor & Francis.

Browne, K., L. Bakshi & J. Lim, (2011), '"It's something you just have to ignore": Understanding and addressing contemporary lesbian, gay, bisexual and trans safety beyond hate crime paradigms', *Journal of Social Policy*, 40(4), 739–56.

Browne, K., N. Banerjea, L. Bakshi & N. McGlynn, (2015), 'Intervention-Gay-Friendly or homophobic? The absence and problems of global standards', *Antipode Online*, 11 May. Available at: https://radicalantipode.wordpress.com/2015/05/11/gay-friendly-or-homophobic/ (accessed 30 May 2022).

Browne, K., N. McGlynn, L. Bakshi & N. Banerjea, (2016), 'Acting on equalities: Are local authorities in England meeting the duties of the Equality Act 2010 and addressing sexual orientation & gender identity?', *University of Brighton*, 7 October. Available at: https://research.brighton.ac.uk/en/publications/acting-on-equalities-are-local-authorities-in-england-meeting-the-2 (accessed 30 May 2022).

Browne, K., N. Banerjea, N. McGlynn, L. Bakshi, R. Banerjee & R. Biswas, (2017), 'Towards transnational feminist queer methodologies', *Gender, Place & Culture*, 24(10), 1376–97.

Browne, K., J. Lim, J. Hall & N. McGlynn, (2021a), 'Sexual (ities that) progress: Introduction', *Environment and Planning C: Politics and Space*, 39(1), 3–10.

Browne, K., N. Banerjea, N. McGlynn, L. Bakshi, S. Beethi & R. Biswas, (2021b), 'The limits of legislative change: Moving beyond inclusion/exclusion to create "a life worth living"', *Environment and Planning C: Politics and Space*, 39(1), 30–52.

Butler, J., (1990), *Gender Trouble: Feminism and the Subversion of Identity*, Routledge.

Butler, J., (1991), 'Disorderly woman', *Transition*, 53, 86–95.

Butler, J., (1993), *Bodies That Matter: On the Discursive Limits of 'Sex'*, Routledge.

Butler, J., (2003), *Giving an Account of Oneself: A Critique of Ethical Violence*, Uitgeverij Van Gorcum.

Butler, J., (2004a), *Undoing Gender*, Routledge.

Butler, J., (2004b), *Precarious Life: The Powers of Mourning and Violence*, Verso.

Butler, J., (2009), *Frames of War: When Is Life Grievable?*, Verso.

Butler, J., (2015), *Notes Toward a Performative Theory of Assembly*, Harvard University Press.

Butler, J., (2016), 'Rethinking vulnerability and resistance', in J. Butler, Z. Gambetti & L. Sabsay (eds.), *Vulnerability in Resistance*, Duke University Press, 12–27.

Butler, J., Gambetti, Z., & L. Sabsay (eds.), (2016), *Vulnerability in Resistance*, Duke University Press.

Chadwick, R., (2017), 'Embodied methodologies: Challenges, reflections and strategies', *Qualitative Research*, 17(1), 54–74.

Clare, E., (2002) 'Sex, celebration, and Justice: A keynote for QD2002', in *Queerness and Disability Conference*, San Francisco.

Conway, D., (2021), 'Whose lifestyle matters at Johannesburg Pride? The lifestylisation of LGBTQ+ identities and the gentrification of activism', *Sociology*, 56(1), 148–65.

Cresswell, T., (1997), 'Weeds, plagues, and bodily secretions: A geographical interpretation of metaphors of displacement', *Annals of the Association of American Geographers*, 87(2), 330–45.

Currah, P., (2013), 'Homonationalism, state rationalities, and sex contradictions', *Theory & Event*, 16(1).

Dahl, U. & J. Gabb, (2019), 'Trends in contemporary queer kinship and family research', *Lambda Nordica*, 24(2–3), 209–37.

Das, V., (2012), 'Ordinary ethics', in D. Fassin (ed.), *A Companion to Moral Anthropology*, Wiley & Sons, 133–49.

Das, V., (2020), *Textures of the Ordinary: Doing Anthropology after Wittgenstein*, Fordham University Press.

Dawney, L., (2013), 'Commoning: The production of common worlds', *Lo Squaderno*, 30, 33–5.

Deswal, D., (2010), 'Now, khaps want ban on gay sex, surrogacy', *The Times of India*, 2 August. Available at: https://timesofindia.indiatimes.com/india/now-khaps-want-ban-on-gay-sex-surrogacy/articleshow/6245847.cms (accessed 30 May 2022).

Devika, J., (2021), 'The kiss of love protests', in P. Kumar (ed.), *Sexuality, Abjection and Queer Existence in Contemporary India*, Routledge, 131–48.

Dhawan, N., (2016), 'Homonationalism and state-phobia: The postcolonial predicament of queering modernities', in M. A. Viteri & M. L. Picq (eds.), *Queering Paradigms V: Queering Narratives of Modernity*, Peter Lang, 51–68.

Di Feliciantonio, C., (2016), 'In Italy it's different: Pride as a space of political contention', in G. Brown & K. Browne (ed.), *The Routledge Research Companion to Geographies of Sex and Sexualities*, Routledge, 121–8.

Domosh, M., (2003), 'Toward a more fully reciprocal feminist inquiry', *ACME: An International Journal for Critical Geographies*, 2(1), 107–11.

Duggan, L., (2002), 'The new homonormativity: The sexual politics of neoliberalism', in R. Castronovo & D. Nelson (eds.), *Materializing Democracy: Toward a Revitalized Cultural Politics*, Duke University Press, 175–94.

Duggan, L., (2003), *The Twilight of Equality?: Neoliberalism, Cultural Politics, and the Attack on Democracy*, Beacon Press.

Dutta, A., (2013), 'Legible identities and legitimate citizens: The globalization of transgender and subjects of HIV-AIDS prevention in Eastern India', *International Feminist Journal of Politics*, 15(4), 494–514.

Dutta, A. & R. Roy, (2014), 'Decolonizing transgender in India: Some reflections', *Transgender Studies Quarterly*, 1(3), 320–37.

Ekine, S., (2016), 'Beyond anti-LGBT legislation: Criminalization and the denial of citizenship', in S. Bakshi, J. Suhraiya & S. Posocco (eds.), *Decolonizing Sexualities. Transnational Perspectives, Critical Interventions*, Counterpress, 19–31.

European Parliament Intergroup on LGBT Rights, (2014), 'European parliament votes for UN development strategy to include LGBTI rights', *European Parliament Intergroup on LGBT Rights*, 26 November. Available at: https://lgbti-ep.eu/2014/11/26/european-parliament-votes-for-development-strategy-to-include-lgbti-rights/ (accessed 30 May 2022).

Falzon, M., (2016), *Multi-sited Ethnography: Theory, Praxis and Locality in Contemporary Research*, Routledge.

Fox, M., (2015), 'Embodied methodologies, participation, and the art of research', *Social and Personality Psychology Compass*, 9(7), 321–32.

Garcia, A. S., (2016), 'Reasons for optimism: Same sex marriage in Mexico city', in S. Bakshi, S. Jivraj & S. Posocco (eds.), ***Decolonizing Sexualities: Transnational Perspectives, Critical Interventions***, Counterpress, 231–48.

García-López, G., (2013), 'Scaling up from the grassroots and the top down: The impacts of multi-level governance on community forestry in Durango, Mexico', *International Journal of the Commons*, 7(2), 406–31.

GEO (2010), 'Equality Act 2010', *Government Equalities Office*. Available at: https://www.legislation.gov.uk/ukpga/2010/15/contents (accessed 30 May 2022).

Goltz, D. B., (2013), 'It gets better: Queer futures, critical frustrations, and radical potentials', *Critical Studies in Media Communication*, 30(2), 135–51.

Gorman-Murray, A. & C. J. Nash, (2014), 'Mobile places, relational spaces: Conceptualizing change in Sydney's LGBTQ neighborhoods', *Environment and Planning D: Society and Space*, 32(4), 622–41.

Gorman-Murray, A. & C. J. Nash, (2017), 'Transformations in LGBT consumer landscapes and leisure spaces in the neoliberal city', *Urban Studies*, 54(3), 786–805.

Halberstam, J., (2005), *In a Queer Time and Place: Transgender Bodies, Subcultural Lives*, NYU Press.

Halberstam, J., (2011), *The Queer Art of Failure*, Duke University Press.

Haraway, D., (1988), 'Situated knowledges: The science question in feminism and the privilege of partial perspective', *Feminist Studies*, 14(3), 575–99.

Harding, R. & E. Peel, (2006), 'We do? International perspectives on equality, legality and same-sex relationships', *Lesbian & Gay Psychology Review*, 7(2), 123–40.

Harding, S. G., (1998), *Is Science Multicultural?: Postcolonialisms, Feminisms, and Epistemologies*, Indiana University Press.

Harvey, D., (2011), 'The future of the commons', *Radical History Review*, 2011(109), 101–7.

Hemmings, C., (2007), 'What's in a name? Bisexuality, transnational sexuality studies and Western colonial legacies', *International Journal of Human Rights*, 11(1–2), 13–32.

Hemmings, C., (2002), *Bisexual Spaces: A Geography of Sexuality and Gender*, Routledge: London.

Hemmings, C., (2013), *Bisexual Spaces: A Geography of Sexuality and Gender*, Routledge.

Herek, G. M., (2002), 'Gender gaps in public opinion about lesbians and gay men', *Public Opinion Quarterly*, 66(1), 40–66.

Herek, G. M., (2009), 'Sexual stigma and sexual prejudice in the United States: A conceptual framework', in D. A. Hope (ed.), *Contemporary Perspectives on Lesbian, Gay, and Bisexual Identities*, Springer, 65–111.

Hubbard, P., (2006), *City*, London: Taylor & Francis.

Hubbard, P., (2008), 'Here, there, everywhere: The ubiquitous geographies of heteronormativity', *Geography Compass*, 2(3), 640–58.

Hubbard, P., (2013), *Cities and Sexualities*, Routledge.

Hubbard, P. & E. Wilkinson, (2015), 'Welcoming the world? Hospitality, homonationalism, and the London 2012 Olympics', *Antipode*, 47(3), 598–615.

ILGA Europe, (2022), 'Rainbow Europe 2015', *ILGA Europe*. Available at: https://www.ilga-europe.org/rainboweurope/2015 (accessed 30 May 2022).

Jivraj, S., S. Bakshi & S. Posocco, (2020), 'Decolonial trajectories: Praxes and challenges', *Interventions*, 22(4), 451–63.

Johnson, K., (2015), *Sexuality: A Psychosocial Manifesto*, John Wiley & Sons.

Johnson, K., P. Faulkner, H. Jones & E. Welsh, (2007), 'Understanding suicidal distress and promoting survival in lesbian, gay, bisexual and transgender (LGBT) communities', *University of Brighton*. Available at: https://citeseerx.ist.psu.edu/viewdoc/download?doi=10.1.1.627.8017&rep=rep1&type=pdf (accessed 30 May 2022).

Johnston, L., (2007), *Queering Tourism: Paradoxical Performances of Gay Pride Parades*, Routledge.

Kallock, S., (2018), 'Livability: A politics for abnormative lives', *Sexualities*, 21(7), 1170–93.

Kaptani, E. & N. Yuval-Davis, (2008), 'Participatory theatre as a research methodology: Identity, performance and social action among refugees', *Sociological Research Online*, 13(5), 1–12.

Karhu, S., (2022), 'Gender skepticism, trans livability, and feminist critique', *Signs: Journal of Women in Culture and Society*, 47(2), 295–317.

Kates, S. M. & R. W. Belk, (2001), 'The meanings of lesbian and gay pride day: Resistance through consumption and resistance to consumption', *Journal of Contemporary Ethnography*, 30(4), 392–429.

Katyal, A., (2016), *The Doubleness of Sexuality: Idioms of Same-Sex Desire in Modern India*, New Text.

Katyal, S. K., (2017), 'The numerus clausus of sex', *University of Chicago Law Review*, 84(1), 389–494.

Kenttamaa Squires, K., (2019), 'Rethinking the homonormative? Lesbian and Hispanic Pride events and the uneven geographies of commoditized identities', *Social & Cultural Geography*, 20(3), 367–86.

Khanna, A., (2013), 'Three hundred and seventy seven ways of being–sexualness of the citizen in India', *Journal of Historical Sociology*, 26(1), 120–42.

Khanna, A., (2016), *Sexualness*, New Text.

Kulpa, R., (2014), 'Western leveraged pedagogy of Central and Eastern Europe: Discourses of homophobia, tolerance, and nationhood', *Gender, Place & Culture*, 21(4), 431–48.

Kulpa, R. & J. Mizielinska (eds.), (2011), *De-centring Western Sexualities: Central and Eastern European Perspectives*, Routledge.

Kulpa, R. & J. M. Silva, (2016), 'Decolonizing queer epistemologies: Section introduction', in G. Brown & K. Browne (eds.), *The Routledge Research Companion to Geographies of Sex and Sexualities*, Routledge, 163–6.

Kumar, A., (2012), 'Khap panchayats: A socio-historical overview', *Economic and Political Weekly*, 47(4), 59–64.

Lalor, K. & K. Browne, (2018), 'Here versus there: Creating British sexual politics elsewhere', *Feminist Legal Studies*, 26(2), 205–13.

Lamusse, T., (2016), 'Politics at pride?', *New Zealand Sociology*, 31(6), 49–70.

Lawrence, M. & Y. Taylor, (2020), 'The UK government LGBT action plan: Discourses of progress, enduring stasis, and LGBTQI+ lives "getting better"', *Critical Social Policy*, 40(4), 586–607.

Lloyd, M., (2015), 'The ethics and politics of vulnerable bodies', in M. Lloyd (ed.), ***Butler and Ethics***, University of Edinburgh Press, 167–92.

Lugones, M., (2010), 'Toward a decolonial feminism', ***Hypatia***, 25(4), 742–59.

Maliepaard, E., (2015), 'Bisexual spaces: Exploring geographies of bisexualities', ***ACME: An International Journal for Critical Geographies***, 14(1), 217–34.

Maliepaard, E., (2017), 'Bisexuality in the Netherlands: Connecting bisexual passing, communities, and identities', ***Journal of Bisexuality***, 17(3), 325–48.

Maliepaard, E., (2020), 'Spaces with a bisexual appearance: Re-conceptualizing bisexual space(s) through a study of bisexual practices in the Netherlands', ***Social & Cultural Geography***, 21(1), 45–63.

Marcus, G. E., (1995), 'Ethnography in/of the world system: The emergence of multi-sited ethnography', ***Annual Review of Anthropology***, 24(1), 95–117.

Marcus, G. E., (2011), 'Multi-sited ethnography: Five or six things I know about it now', in Simon Coleman, Pauline von Hellermann (eds.), ***Multi-sited Ethnography: Problems and Possibilties in the Translocation of Research Methods***, Routledge, 24–40.

Matthews, P., (2020), 'Debate: LGBTQ rights in public services – a battle won?', ***Public Money & Management***, 40(6), 423–5.

McCarter, R., (2008), 'Common sense: Toward an architecture both poetic and practical', in B. Healy (ed.), ***Commonplaces: Thinking About and American Architecture***, ORO Editions, 6–13.

McGlynn, N., (2018), 'Slippery geographies of the urban and the rural: Public sector LGBT equalities work in the shadow of the "Gay Capital"', ***Journal of Rural Studies***, 57(1), 65–77.

McGlynn, N., K. Browne, N. Banerjea, R. Biswas, S. Banerjee & L. Bakshi, (2020), 'More than happiness: Aliveness and struggle in lesbian, gay, bisexual, trans and queer lives', ***Sexualities***, 23(7), 1113–34.

Mignolo, W., (2000), ***Local Histories/Global Designs: Coloniality, Subaltern Knowledges, and Border Thinking***, Princeton University Press.

Mignolo, W., (2016), 'Foreword: Decolonial body-geo-politics at large', in S. Bakshi, S. Jivraj & S. Posocco (eds.), *Decolonizing Sexualities: Transnational Perspectives, Critical Interventions*, Counterpress, vii–xviii.

Mignolo, W., (2011a), *The Darker Side of Western Modernity*, Duke University Press.

Mignolo, W., (2011b), 'Epistemic disobedience and the decolonial option: A manifesto', *Transmodernity*, 1(2), 3–23.

Mizielińska, J., J. Gabb & A. Stasińska, (2018), 'Editorial introduction to special issue: Queer kinship and relationships', *Sexualities*, 21(7), 975–82.

Monk, J. & S. Hanson, (1982), 'On not excluding half of the human in human geography', *The Professional Geographer*, 34(1), 11–23.

Monro, S. & D. Richardson, (2014), 'Lesbian, gay and bisexual populations: The role of English local government', *Local Government Studies*, 40(6), 869–87.

Moosavi, L., (2020), 'The decolonial bandwagon and the dangers of intellectual decolonisation', *International Review of Sociology*, 30(2), 332–54.

Moran, L., (2002), *The Homosexual(ity) of Law*, Routledge.

Morgensen, S. L., (2010), 'Settler homonationalism: Theorizing settler colonialism within queer modernities', *GLQ: A Journal of Lesbian and Gay Studies*, 16(1–2), 105–31.

Mudur, G. S., (2013), 'Gay sex law raises mental health fears', *The Telegraph India*, 15 December. Available at: https://www.telegraphindia.com/india/gay-sex-law-raises-mental-health-fears/cid/231259 (accessed 30 May 2022).

Munoz, J., (2009), *Cruising Utopia: The Then and There of Queer Futurity*, NYU Press.

Nagar, R., (2019), 'Hungry translations: The world through radical vulnerability: The 2017 antipode RGS-IBG lecture', *Antipode*, 51(1), 3–24.

Nash, C. J., (2013), 'The age of the "post-mo"? Toronto's gay village and a new generation', *Geoforum*, 49, 243–52.

Nash, C. J. & A. Gorman-Murray, (2014), 'LGBT neighbourhoods and "new mobilities": Towards understanding transformations in sexual and gendered urban landscapes', *International Journal of Urban and Regional Research*, 38(3), 756–72.

Nash, C. J. & A. Gorman-Murray, (2015), 'Lesbians in the city: Mobilities and relational geographies', *Journal of Lesbian Studies*, 19(2), 173–91.

Nash, C. J. & K. Browne, (2020), **Heteroactivism: Resisting Lesbian, Gay, Bisexual and Trans Rights and Equalities**, Bloomsbury Publishing.

NDTV, (2011), 'Ghulam Nabi Azad calls homosexuality "unnatural" and a "disease"', *NDTV*, 5 July. Available at: https://www.ndtv.com/india-news/ghulam-nabi-azad-calls-homosexuality-unnatural-and-a-disease-460367 (accessed 30 May 2022).

Nunez, C., (2017), 'Where dating apps save lives', *National Geographic*, 15 May. Available at: https://www.nationalgeographic.com/culture/article/grindr-health-safety-security-lgbt-community-india (accessed 30 May 2022).

O'Brien, J., (2008), 'Afterword: Complicating homophobia', *Sexualities*, 11(4), 496–512.

Ostrom, E., (1990), **Governing the Commons: The Evolution of Institutions for Collective Action**, Cambridge University Press.

Oswin, N., (2007), 'Producing homonormativity in neoliberal South Africa: Recognition, redistribution, and the equality project', *Signs: Journal of Women in Culture and Society*, 32(3), 649–69.

Patil, V., (2018), 'The heterosexual matrix as imperial effect', *Sociological Theory*, 36(1), 1–26.

Pattanaik, D., (2013), 'Is it Hindu to be homophobic?', *The Times of India*, 15 December. Available at: https://timesofindia.indiatimes.com/home/sunday-times/deep-focus/is-it-hindu-to-be-homophobic/articleshow/27387444.cms (accessed 30 May 2022).

Pattanaik, D., (2019, January), 'The LGBTQ Movement in India', *Seminar*, 713, 104–7.

Perry, B., (2002), **In the Name of Hate: Understanding Hate Crimes**, Routledge.

Pisharoty, S. B., (2013), 'It is like reversing the motion of the Earth', *The Hindu*, 20 December. Available at: https://www.thehindu.com/features/metroplus/society/it-is-like-reversing-the-motion-of-the-earth/article5483306.ece (accessed 30 May 2022).

Plaut, M., (2014), 'Uganda donors cut aid after president passes anti-gay law', *The Guardian*, 25 February. Available at: https://www.theguardian.com/global-development/2014/feb/25/uganda-donors-cut-aid-anti-gay-law (accessed 30 May 2022).

Ponniah, U. & S. Tamalapakula, (2020), 'Caste-ing queer identities', *NUJS Law Review*, 13(3), 1–8.

Posocco, S., (2016), '(Decolonizing) the ear of the other: Subjectivity, ethics and politics in question', in S. Bakshi, S. Jivraj & S. Posocco (eds.), *Decolonizing Sexualities: Transnational Perspectives, Critical Interventions*, Counterpress, 249–63.

Puar, J., (2013), 'Rethinking homonationalism', *International Journal of Middle East Studies*, 45(2), 336–9.

Puar, J., (2007), *Terrorist Assemblages*, Duke University Press.

Rao, R., (2014), 'The locations of homophobia', *London Review of International Law*, 2(2), 169–99.

Rao, R., (2020), *Out of Time: The Queer Politics of Postcoloniality*, Oxford University Press.

Revathi, A., (2016), *A Life in Trans Activism*, Zubaan.

Richardson, D., (2004), 'Locating sexualities: From here to normality', *Sexualities*, 7(4), 391–411.

Richardson, D., (2005), 'Desiring sameness? The rise of a neoliberal politics of normalisation', *Antipode*, 37(3), 515–35.

Richardson, D., (2017), 'Rethinking sexual citizenship', *Sociology*, 51(2), 208–24.

Richardson, D. & S. Monro, (2012), *Sexuality, Equality and Diversity*, Macmillan International Higher Education.

Rivers, I., C. Gonzalez, N. Nodin, E. Peel & A. Tyler, (2018), 'LGBT people and suicidality in youth: A qualitative study of perceptions of risk and protective circumstances', *Social Science & Medicine*, 212, 1–8.

Rodríguez, J. M., (2014), *Sexual Futures, Queer Gestures, and Other Latina Longings*, NYU Press.

Rose, G., (1993), *Feminism & Geography: The Limits of Geographical Knowledge*, University of Minnesota Press.

Rushing, S., (2010), 'Preparing for politics: Judith Butler's ethical dispositions', *Contemporary Political Theory*, 9(3), 284–303.

Sabsay, L., (2012), 'The emergence of the other sexual citizen: Orientalism and the modernisation of sexuality', *Citizenship Studies*, 16(5–6), 605–23.

Said, E., (1978), ***Orientalism***, Pantheon Books.

Santos, A., (2012), ***Social Movements and Sexual Citizenship in Southern Europe***, Springer.

Santos, A. C., (2013), 'Are we there yet? Queer sexual encounters, legal recognition and homonormativity', *Journal of Gender Studies*, 22(1), 54–64.

Scott, J. W., (2013), 'Experience', in J. Butler & J. W. Scott (eds.), ***Feminists Theorize the Political***, Routledge, 40–58.

Sears, A., (2005), 'Queer anti-capitalism: What's left of lesbian and gay liberation?', *Science & Society*, 69(1), 92–112.

Sedgewick, E., (2003), ***Touching Feeling: Affect, Pedagogy***, Duke University Press.

Sharma, G. & R. Kaul, (2009), 'Blood banks outlaw gay donors despite shortages', *Hindustan Times*, 15 July. Available at: https://www.hindustantimes.com/india/blood-banks-outlaw-gay-donors-despite-shortages/story-WgM8CYz87QGlFImvdChuMJ.html (accessed 30 May 2022).

Silva, J. M. & M. J. Ornat, (2016), '"Wake up, Alice, this is not wonderland!" Power, diversity and knowledge in geographies of sexualities', in G. Brown & K. Browne (eds.), ***The Routledge Research Companion to Geographies of Sex and Sexualities***, Routledge, 209–16.

Sircar, O., (2021), 'A brief prehistory of queer freedom in the New India', in P. Kumar (ed.), ***Sexuality, Abjection and Queer Existence in Contemporary India***, Routledge, 226–50.

Sircar, O. & D. Jain, (2017), ***New Intimacies, Old Desires: Law, Culture and Queer Politics in Neoliberal Times***, Zubaan New Delhi.

Stanley, L. & S. Wise, (1983), ***Breaking Out: Feminist Consciousness and Feminist Research***, Routledge.

Strasser, M., (2014), 'Top twelve most homophobic nations', *Newsweek*, 27 February. Available at: https://www.newsweek.com/top-twelve-most-homophobic-nations-230348 (accessed 30 May 2022).

Stychin, C., (2003), ***Governing Sexuality: The Changing Politics of Citizenship and Law Reform***, Hart Publishing.

Taylor, Y., S. Hines & M. Casey, (2010), *Theorizing Intersectionality and Sexuality*, Springer.

Times of India (2010), 'Mizo church warning to homosexuals', *The Times of India*, 6 June. Available at: https://timesofindia.indiatimes.com/india/mizo-church-warning-to-homosexuals/articleshow/6016334.cms (accessed 30 May 2022).

Tyson, J. (2014), 'The world bank's uneasy relationship with LGBTI rights', *Devex*, 21 November. Available at: https://www.devex.com/news/the-world-bank-s-uneasy-relationship-with-lgbti-rights-84896 (accessed 30 May 2022).

Taylor, Y., Hines, S. & M. Casey, (2012), *Theorising Intersectionality and Sexuality*, Palgrave & Macmillan.

Vahanvati, G. E., (2013), 'Law can't remain static: Government told SC that Section 377 didn't reflect Indian values', *The Times of India*, 13 December. Available at: https://timesofindia.indiatimes.com/edit-page/law-cant-remain-static-government-told-sc-that-section-377-didnt-reflect-indian-values/articleshow/27246846.cms (accessed 30 May 2022).

Vanderbeck, R. M., (2005), 'Masculinities and fieldwork: Widening the discussion', *Gender, Place & Culture*, 12(4), 387–402.

Vanita, R., (2011), 'Happily non-married', *Hindustan Times*, 20 November. Available at: https://www.hindustantimes.com/india/happily-non-married/story-qQ70D8I8Ysva8wUedk836N.html (accessed 30 May 2022).

Vanita, R., (2005), *Love's Rite: Same-sex Marriage in India and the West*, Springer.

Vanita, R. & S. Kidwai, (2000), *Same-sex Love in India: Readings in Indian Literature*, Springer.

Warner, M., (1991), 'Introduction: Fear of a queer planet', *Social Text*, 29, 3–17.

Warner, M., (1999a), 'Normal and normaller: Beyond gay marriage', *GLQ: A Journal of Lesbian and Gay Studies*, 5(2), 119–71.

Warner, M., (1999b), *The Trouble with Normal: Sex, Politics, and the Ethics of Queer Life*, Harvard University Press.

Weeks, J., (2007), *The World We Have Won: The Remaking of Erotic and Intimate Life*, Routledge.

Wilkinson, E., (2012), 'The romantic imaginary: Compulsory coupledom and single existence', in S. Hines & Y. Taylor (eds.), *Sexualities: Past Reflections, Future Directions*, Springer, 130–45.

Wilkinson, E., (2020), 'Never after? Queer temporalities and the politics of non-reproduction', *Gender, Place & Culture*, 27(5), 660–76.

Yengkhom, S., (2009), 'Spurt in AIDS cases in gay community', *The Times of India*, 1 December. Available at: https://timesofindia.indiatimes.com/city/kolkata/spurt-in-aids-cases-in-gay-community/articleshow/5286263.cms (accessed 30 May 2022).

Index

academic knowledge production 51
academic writing 40, 52
activism 11, 18, 30–1, 35, 42, 51–3, 56, 63–4, 91–2
   activist collaborations 37, 50–6
   community 139
   politico-cultural 126
adoption and parental rights 4, 54, 72
advertisements 27, 131, 146
Africa 57–9
amar benche thaka (my living) 112
Amar Bhasha Amar Bhashya (*I will script my script*) chant 142
andolon (movement) 112, 120–1
Anglo-American 10, 36, 39, 63, 162 n.2
anondo (happiness) 112
Anti-Homosexuality Bill of Uganda 48
Articles of the Constitution of India 74, 162 n.6
assimilation/assimilationist 12–13, 48, 63, 112, 114, 120

Bacchetta, P. 42
Bakshi, L. 13, 31, 51–2, 95, 115
   on Liveable Lives 153–4
Banerjea, N. 38–40, 132, 138, 145, 149, 160 nn.2–3, 161 n.9
Banerjee, R. 51, 138, 159, 163 n.15
Bangladesh 156–8
   Bangla transliterations 17, 26–7, 54, 120, 139, 156, 161 n.8, 167 n.7
   Dhaka 158–9
bearable 34, 40, 58–9, 116
becoming normal 13, 81, 95, 108, 112, 115, 130, 151
Beethi, S. 51
benche thaka (to live) 54, 99, 121

benche thaka ebong tike thaka (to live and to survive) 24, 30, 96–108, 121–2. *See also* liveability/liveabilities; surviving/survival
bhalo thaka (staying well) 17, 24, 53–4
bhalo thaka ebong kharap thaka (staying well/unwell) 24
bhalobasa (love) 112
Bharatiya Janata Party (BJP) 73, 165 nn.11–12
bigotry 77
bio-politics/biopower 163 n.10
bisexual 27, 53, 87–9, 109, 160 n.2
Biswas, R. 51
body-politics 46, 163 n.10
Brahmanical norms 12, 65, 162 n.2
break the silence 53–4
Brighton Pride (2016) 60
British Queer 29, 37, 43–6, 58, 60, 63. *See also* Indian Queer; queer
Brown, G. 10
Browne, K. 3, 13, 39–40, 95, 115, 132, 149, 160 n.3
Butler, J. 2, 6
   good life 32–3
   and liveability 6–10, 14–15, 32, 56
   on living and surviving 106
   normative commitment to equality 14–15
   Notes toward a Performative Theory of Assembly 97
   order of being 110
   Undoing Gender 15, 96

capitalism 40
caste 5, 10, 12, 38, 40, 42, 55, 65, 71–2, 79, 89, 108, 112, 114, 162 n.4, 162 n.6, 167 n.10

caste-based territorial social groups 164 n.4
Chandrachud, D. Y. 163 n.9
cisgender 13, 38, 109, 119, 140, 165 n.9
civil partnerships 68, 157
civilization 43, 63, 68, 84
Clare, E., queer crip theory 13–14
class 10, 12, 38, 42, 72, 79, 89, 108, 112, 114, 138–9, 156, 167 n.10
collage making project 22–3
colonial/coloniality 4–5, 36–8, 40–50, 52, 56, 62–4. *See also* decolonial/decoloniality; postcolonial
  colonial difference 35, 45–6, 49, 52, 56–7, 63
  colonial matrix of power 40, 48, 163 n.13
commercial/commercialization 60, 125–6, 138
common-sense norms 75, 77, 127, 129
commonplace 17, 31, 125, 131, 150
  commoning 128, 143, 148
  loss of urban commons 128
  politics 127–9
  temples in India 166 n.3
  temporary commons 129
community activism 139
comparative methodologies 17–18, 22, 44, 46, 58, 63, 68, 131
Congress party (Indian National Congress) 73, 165 n.12
consensual sexual acts 46, 73, 161 n.11
Covid pandemic (lockdown) 2, 31, 39–40, 156
CPI(M) (Communist Party of India(Marxist)) 165 n.12
criminalization of homosexuality 162 n.6
culture/cultural 2–3, 19, 26, 37, 41–3, 47, 61, 75, 84, 104, 166 n.1

Das, V., ordinary ethics 16
Dawney, L. 128
Debalina 131, 145
  Ebong Bewarish 164 n.17
  interviews with participants 148
decolonial/decoloniality 4–5, 19, 26, 28–9, 32–3, 35–7, 40–1, 45, 50–1, 55–6, 60–1, 63, 65, 71, 130
decriminalization 19, 46–7. *See also* recriminalization
democratic system 3–4. *See also* Western democracies
Denmark 48
discrimination 9, 15, 53, 60, 62, 71, 79, 91–3, 102, 116, 120, 123, 139–41, 163 n.8
dispossession 48, 52, 96
duhsahosik abhijan (daring adventure) 112

Eastern Europe 59
embodied methodology 130–1
emotion/emotional 53, 75, 106, 114, 139, 141, 146, 150
England 18–20, 24, 26, 51, 59–60, 66, 68, 70, 78, 91–2, 151, 161 n.13
  Brighton 1, 18, 25, 31, 39, 51, 125, 129–32, 151–2, 154–9, 167 n.11
  performing liveabilities in 144–50
  Equalities Legislation report 25
  Equality Impact Assessments 166 n.14
  LGBTQ recognition and equality in 75–84
  project workshop in 24–5, 27, 59, 75–7, 80–7
    collage making 22–3
    Franco's 79–80
    on normative/non-normative 110–11
    on ordinary and the everyday 115–18, 122

186　Index

on survival and living 5, 97–8, 102–6
public sector funding 69
same-sex Marriage Act 46, 66, 162 n.8
websites for local authorities in 164 n.2
Enlightenment 162 n.2
epistemic disobedience 51, 163 n.13
epistemology/epistemological 2, 6, 41, 44–5, 57, 125–6, 166 n.1 (Ch 4)
equalities 1–2, 4, 14, 19, 29, 37, 41, 43, 47, 53, 63, 115, 126, 150, 164 n.2
　equalities legislation 2, 4, 19–20, 25, 29, 43, 65–70, 88–9, 91–2, 110, 127, 160 n.4
　of LGBTQ in India and UK 75–84
　marriage equality rights 155, 157
Equality Act (2010) 19, 29, 66–7, 162–3 n.8, 164 n.2, 166 n.14
　councils 67–8
　Equality Impact Assessments 166 n.14
　Equality Objective 67
　Specific Duties Regulations 2011 67
ethics/ethical 7, 15–16, 51, 54, 116
　ethics of inclusion 85–6
ethnic/ethnicity 12, 104, 112, 147
Eurocentric/Eurocentrism 37, 162 n.2
European Court of Human Rights 19
European Parliament Intergroup on LGBT Rights (2014) 48

family acceptances 90
feminist 17, 38, 40, 42, 51, 54, 163 n.14
forward/backward 1–2, 18, 21, 29, 32, 35, 37, 41, 50, 55, 61, 70. See also progress/backwardness

　recognition and rights in backward states 70–4
Franco's map, project workshop 58–60
freedom 4, 35, 50, 65, 112, 155

gay 10, 43, 71–2, 76, 80, 142, 151
　ban from donating blood in England 165 n.5
gender. See sexuality/gendered practices
geographies/geographical 20, 25, 40, 161 n.13, 162 n.1
　imaginations/imaginings 2–4, 37, 44, 47, 56–62
　other places 29, 43, 56–62, 151
　of sexualities 57, 125
geopolitics/geopolitical 3–4, 11, 18, 30, 33, 43–4, 57–8, 62, 64, 89, 95, 158
Global North and Global South 3, 18–20, 26–30, 36–7, 44–9, 55, 57, 62, 157, 162 n.2
Government Equalities Office (GEO) 67, 164 n.2
Great Britain 19–20, 28–9, 32, 37, 44, 47–9, 66, 81, 161 n.13, 162 n.8
Guha, P. 166 n.1 (Ch 5)

Halberstam, J. 115
Harvey, D. 128
Hashmi, S. 166 n.1 (Ch 5)
hate crimes 43, 80
hegemonic 1–2, 13, 41, 45, 63, 109, 166 n.1 (Ch 4)
heteronormative/heteronormativity 10, 13, 29, 39, 61, 77, 95–6, 104, 116, 119–20, 125, 127, 158
heteropatriarchal 12, 41, 43, 53
heterosexual/heterosexuality 15, 42, 87, 142, 166 n.1 (Ch 4), 167 n.10

Index

heterosexual marriage 109, 111
heterosexual matrix 15, 107, 166 nn.1–2 (Ch 4)
hierarchies/hierarchization 3, 15, 19–20, 27, 29, 43–4, 47, 55, 62, 66, 101, 122
   hierarchies of needs 99, 101
Hindu Marriage Act (1955) 165 n.7
Hindu/Hinduism 42, 71–2, 161 n.7
   same-sex love and 72, 165 n.8
HIV/AIDS awareness 71
homoerotic/homoeroticism 71, 165 n.6
homonormative/homonormativity 10, 12, 16, 29, 43, 68, 114, 126–7, 158
homophobia/homophobic 18–20, 46–8, 59–60, 62, 80, 92
homosexual/homosexuality 19, 41–2, 47, 60, 71–2, 164 n.4
   criminalization of 162 n.6

identity twister game 147–8
ILGA Europe rainbow list 69
imaginations 3–4, 10, 42, 54–6, 125, 128, 130–1
inclusion/exclusion legislation 10–12, 17, 29, 31, 33, 47–9, 65, 75, 89, 91–2, 110, 127, 160 n.4
India 12, 18–20, 24, 26, 29, 32, 37–8, 42, 44–5, 47–9, 51, 57–8, 70, 91–2, 154, 161 n.12
   activisms in 64
   Delhi 2, 16, 18, 71
   India Media analysis 60–1
   Kerala 161 n.7
   Khajuraho and Konarak temples 71, 165 n.6
   Khap panchayats in 164 n.4
   Kolkata 1, 18, 25, 31, 51, 112, 120, 125–6, 129–32, 146, 151–2, 154–9
      performing liveabilities in 132–44
   Ranuchhaya Arena 138, 142
   Y Channel, Esplanade 138, 141
   LBTQ in 27
   LGBTQ recognition and equality in 75–84
   media analysis 29–30
   Mizoram 72
   northwest 71, 164 n.4
   participants interview
      LGBTQ people 76–9, 86, 90–1
      on living and surviving 5, 100–2, 104, 109
      on normative/non-normative 113–14
      on ordinary and the everyday 115, 118–20
   project workshop in 61, 76–8, 83, 87–90
      collage making 22–3
      on normative/non-normative 110, 112–13
      on ordinary and the everyday 116–17, 121
      on survival and living 99–100, 106
   unrecorded names 165 n.13
   queer feminists in 54
   right-wing in 42, 48, 88–9, 161 n.7, 165 n.11
   temples in 166 n.3 (Ch 4)
   West Bengal 25, 76, 78, 83, 113, 151, 156, 158–9, 161 n.13, 167 n.9
Indian Queer 29, 37, 41–2, 44, 63. *See also* British Queer; queer
intelligibility 11, 49, 64, 88, 108, 166 n.1
international human rights and development 3
intersectional/intersectionality 56, 104, 148, 156, 159
Ireland 19
   Dublin 2
   same-sex marriage in 39

Italy 58–9
item numbers (Bollywood songs) 131, 138, 166 n.4

Jawan (soldier) 165 n.10
jeeboner mato jeebon (a life that is like a life) 1, 6, 17, 24, 53–4
juridico-political 2–5, 8, 10–11, 17, 29–30, 32–3, 43–4, 49, 55–7, 60–1, 64, 66, 70, 74–5, 84, 88–9, 91–2, 131, 160 n.4

Kaptani, E. 130
Khanwilkar, A. M. 163 n.9
Kidwai, S. 165 n.6
kins/kinship 39, 54, 64, 86, 114
Kiss of Love protest 12, 161 n.7
Koushal, S. 72–3

language 16, 54, 63, 70, 139, 146–7, 167 n.10
legal cases. *See specific cases*
legal reforms 4, 9, 17, 30, 49, 53–7, 70, 74, 92, 114
legislation(s) 1–5, 8, 10, 22, 37, 41, 46–7, 50, 57, 60, 75, 95
  complex significance of 88–91
  equalities legislation 2, 4, 19–20, 29, 43, 60–1, 65–70, 88–9, 91–2, 110, 127, 160 n.4
  inclusive/exclusive 10–12, 17, 29, 31, 33, 47–9, 65, 75, 89, 91–2, 114
  legislative changes 19, 30, 65–7, 74–5, 79, 81, 85, 87–8, 90–1, 93, 98, 114
  legislative recognition 5, 7–8, 11–12, 30, 34, 45, 70–4, 76, 160 n.6
  legislative reforms 4, 25, 28, 57, 92
  LGBTQ-friendly 19, 71
  Specific Duties of the Public Sector 67
lesbian 27, 39, 53, 72, 76, 109, 138, 140–1, 143, 156, 158–9, 160 n.2, 166 n.15

Lesbian, Gay, Bi, Trans, and Queer (LGBTQ) 1–3, 5, 13, 17, 19–20, 22, 24–9, 32, 44–5, 47–50, 55–61, 66, 71–3, 95–6, 99, 108, 114, 117, 127, 129–30, 139, 147, 150, 160 n.6, 161 n.14, 163 n.8, 166 n.15
  legislative equalities (*see* legislation(s), equalities legislation)
  participants interview 76–9, 86, 90–1
  and political parties 73–4
  politics 20, 60, 62, 142
  project workshops in England and India 22–3, 61, 75–85
  recognition and equality in India and the UK 75–84
LGBT 13, 26–7, 29, 58–62, 104, 149, 162 n.7
LGBTQI movement 157
liberation 4, 10, 16, 29, 64, 160 n.6
live music 140
liveability/liveabilities 1–6, 16–17, 24–6, 32–4, 50–6, 58, 60, 62–4, 66, 74, 83, 88–9, 95–6, 100, 104, 108, 111, 114, 118, 122–3, 126, 129–31, 151, 153, 155–8
  and Butler 6–10, 14–15, 32, 56
  and decoloniality (*see* decolonial/decoloniality)
  normative/non-normative 30, 96, 107–15, 122–3, 155 (*see also* non-normative; normative/normativity)
  performing liveabilities
    in Brighton 144–50
    in Kolkata 132–44
  and survival 96–108, 121–3, 130–1, 158
  transnational-methodological research 2, 17–28
lived experiences 6, 11, 32, 44, 54, 66, 79, 131, 146

Index

local government 25, 29, 67–9, 164 n.2

macro-geographical imaginings 56
mainstream 11, 16, 22, 48, 101, 141, 143, 167 n.10
Making Liveable Lives: Rethinking Social Exclusion 1–2, 44
    data collection methods 21–2
Malhotra, I. 163 n.9
Malobika, Minakshi Sanyal 156–7
maps 58, 162 n.1, 164 n.16
marginalization 5, 43, 48, 53, 55–6, 60, 62, 69, 72, 75–6, 88, 95, 122, 146
marriage 109–10
    heterosexual 109, 111
    marriage equality 155, 157
    monogamous couple 43, 114
    pressures 90, 109–10, 112
    same-sex (*see* same-sex marriage)
    Vedic Hindu traditions of 165 n.7
Marriage (same-sex couples) Act 46, 66, 162 n.8
material and discursive realities 30, 109, 123
McCarter, R. 127
McGlynn, N. 51
The Middle East 58
Mignolo, W. 163 nn.10–12
    enactment of classification 38
    epistemic disobedience 51, 163 n.13
Misra, D. 163 n.9
modernity 38, 40–1, 63
monogamous couple 43, 114
Monologue – lesbian narratives from Bangladesh and West Bengal 156–8
Mukhopadhaya, S. J. 162 n.7
Munoz, J. 100
Murlidhar, S. 162 n.6
Museveni, Y. 48
Muslim 42, 72

Nariman, R. F. 163 n.9
nation-states 3, 28, 36, 44, 46–7, 55, 62, 67
National Legal Services Authority (NALSA) v Union of India 161 n.12
Nautanki (in Bihar, Uttar Pradesh) genre 140
Navtej Singh Johar and Others vs Union of India case 46, 161 n.11
Naz Foundation vs Government of NCT of Delhi case 19, 46, 70–1, 74, 164 n.4
neeti (values, morals) 120–1
neoliberal 39, 67, 128
New Labour 66
Niyomtantrik ebong niyombirodhee (normative and non-normative) 30, 96, 107–15, 122–3. *See also* non-normative; normative/normativity
non-normative 4–5, 26, 30, 33–4, 95–6, 107–16, 122
normalizations 9–10, 13–16, 29, 65, 68, 92, 95, 114, 116, 122–3
normative/normativity 2, 7–8, 10, 12–17, 22, 30, 33–4, 42, 45, 50, 53, 61, 69, 71, 85, 87–8, 95–6, 99, 107–16, 122–3, 129, 155, 157
    of commercialization 125
    normative violence 53, 85, 108
Norway 48

oppression/oppressive 3, 10, 14, 16, 36, 75, 88, 93, 120, 126, 166 n.1 (Ch 5)
ordinary/ordinariness 6, 12–17, 33, 95, 115, 122, 127, 129
    and the everyday 115–21, 123 (*see also sadharon ar gotanugotik*)
    ordinary ethics 16

ordinary lifeworlds 15–16, 35, 56
  possibilities of 33, 95, 123, 125
Ornat, M. J. 57
others 12, 15, 20, 43–4, 47, 61, 104, 122, 152, 163 n.8
  intimate/non-intimate 143–4
  other places 29, 43, 56–62, 151

peno-vaginal acts 46, 161 n.11
persistence 96–7
political ecology 128
politico-cultural activism 126
popular culture 84
postcolonial 26, 36–7, 42, 89, 107, 161 n.14. *See also* colonial/coloniality; decolonial/decoloniality
  legalities 70–4
power relations 27, 29–30, 36, 38, 40, 43, 51–2, 54–6, 62, 64, 104, 107, 128, 160 n.4, 162 n.2
precarity 7, 9–10, 14–15, 33, 35, 56, 62, 106–7
pride events 125–6
progress/backwardness narratives 2, 18, 27–8, 44, 47, 49–50, 56, 61, 63, 65–70. *See also* forward/backward narratives
protest(s) 12, 72, 120–1, 126–7, 138, 156, 161 n.7
protibad. *See* protest(s)

queer 1, 10–12, 22, 26–7, 33, 35–6, 38–9, 42, 46, 49, 51, 54–6, 63, 71, 107, 138, 143, 146, 148, 155–7, 163 n.14. *See also* British Queer; Indian Queer
  queer feminists in India 54
  temporalities 119
queer woman 38
queerphilia 42, 48
queerphobia/queerphobic 36, 42, 45, 47–9

race/racism/racialized 5, 10, 12, 39–40, 46–7, 55–6, 102, 112, 114, 116, 147, 156, 162 n.6
rationality 11, 45, 64
re-existence 51, 163 n.12
recriminalization 19, 47, 60, 72, 161 n.12. *See also* decriminalization
relationality/relationalities 19, 29, 51, 54, 86, 125–6, 132
religions 55, 72, 108, 162 n.6. *See also specific religions*
resistance 7, 139, 141, 143, 146
Rodriguez, J. M. 92
roopantorkamee (person desiring change) 27
Rushing, S. 15

Sabsay, L. 47
sadharon ar gotanugotik (ordinary and the everyday) 30, 96, 115–21, 123
samakamee naree (woman who desires the same) 38
samakamee (person who desires the same) 27, 142. *See also* queer
same-sex couples 12, 64, 72, 141, 154–5, 157
same-sex marriage 4, 19, 30, 39, 43, 46, 50, 68–9, 72, 75, 81, 84–8, 92, 110, 114, 142, 165 nn.8–9
  ethics of inclusion 85–6
  Koushal on 72–3
  participants interview 86
  project workshop in England 84–5
  and religious considerations 72
Sappho for Equality 1, 25, 27, 51, 53–4, 130–1, 139, 143–4, 156–7, 160 n.2, 164 n.17
  queer feminist politics 54
Sarkar, B. 166 n.1 (Ch 5)

Index

Scheduled Caste 42, 162 n.4.
  See also caste
Scotland 19
Scott, J. W. 6
Section 377 of the Indian Penal Code
    (S 377) 19, 30, 45–6, 53, 66, 70,
    89, 141, 156–7, 161 n.11, 162
    n.6, 163 n.9
  2013 reinstatement of 74
  Koushal on 73
Sedgewick, E. 115
self-identification 116, 119
sexuality/gendered practices 1–5, 7–8,
    10, 12, 16, 26–8, 35–7, 40–2,
    45–6, 49, 55, 57, 62, 65–7, 77,
    95, 97, 107–8, 127, 141, 146–7,
    156, 162 n.6, 162 n.8
  gender reassignment 67
  geographies of sexualities 57
  politics 1–2, 10, 19, 47, 55, 60–2,
    64, 126, 151, 153
  rights and equalities 1–3, 5, 20,
    27, 29, 36–7, 41, 46, 48
  sexual orientation 67, 147
  sexuality rights discourse 20, 27, 62
Shah, A. P. 162 n.6
sharing stories 143, 146
Silva, J. M. 57
Singhvi, G. S. 162 n.7
social change 72, 126, 150
social groups 3, 7, 162 n.4, 164 n.4
social relations 32, 88
South-East Asia 58
srishti (creation) 112
street theatre 18, 22, 28, 31, 50, 123,
    125, 128, 130–2, 151. *See also*
    theatre workshops
  in Brighton 126–7, 129–30,
    144–50
  embodied methodology 130–1
  in Kolkata 126–7, 129–30, 132–44
  performers and onlookers 125–6,
    129–31, 139, 142, 147, 151
subjectification 97, 108

suicides 72, 138
Sumita, B. 31, 52, 130, 138, 140, 146,
    153, 166 n.2 (Ch 5)
  on Liveable Lives 154–9
Suresh Kumar Kaushal vs Naz
    Foundation case 46
surviving/survival 1, 6, 16, 24, 30,
    34, 106
  basic needs 98, 119
  and living 96–108, 121–3, 130–1,
    158
swadhinata (freedom) 112. *See also*
    freedom

Tanzania 48
temporal/temporality 2–4, 15, 35, 47,
    49, 119, 126, 132, 151, 160 n.5
  normative 99–101
  queer 119
theatre workshops 31, 130, 143,
    146, 155. *See also* street theatre
trans-heterosexual 119–20
trans-people/transman 27, 61, 67,
    71–3, 113, 141, 143, 146, 148,
    157, 161 n.12
Transgender Persons' Act 157
transgression/ transgressive 10,
    12–13, 16, 108
transmasculine 53, 138–41, 160 n.2,
    165 n.9
transnational 1–2, 17–18, 20, 24, 27,
    31, 33, 36–7, 44, 49–52, 62, 75,
    126, 131–2, 142, 154, 157–8,
    163 n.14
transnegativity 116

Uganda 48
The United Kingdom. *See* England;
    Great Britain
The United States 38
  Evansville 18

Vahanvati, G. E. 74
Vanita, R. 71, 165 n.6

violations 16, 53, 97, 108, 141, 162 n.6
violence 3, 8, 15, 33, 53, 60, 71–2, 77–9, 92, 97, 102, 108–9, 123, 139–41, 143, 158, 165 n.9
vulnerability 7, 15, 49, 79

Wales 19, 25, 46, 68, 91
Western democracies 20, 47, 62

xenophobia/xenophobic 36, 42, 45, 47–9

Yakshagana (in Karnataka/south India) genre 140
Yatra (in West Bengal) genre 140
Yuval-Davis, N. 130